# The Investors Mindset: Mastering the Wealth Code by Unveiling Untapped Potential

## By: Mustafa Nejem

# Table of Content

# Introduction to the Book

"The Investors Mindset" is a book that will change your mind about how you invest.

Get into the obscurity surrounding venture capital mechanics and figure out the nuances associated with angel investing. Find out what it takes to value a company or negotiate term sheets. It provides insights into due diligence processes that open the doors towards successful funding.

As you move through the book, discover why traction is vital to having a sound business model without exposing your cards too early. This book will help readers understand ways of curbing risks, carry out market analysis and a myriad of other strategies to outpace the competition. Begin a new journey in investing today.

# Chapter 1

# The Investor's Perspective

## The Purpose of an Investor

Understanding the investor's objectives is crucial when you are starting the journey towards financial independence. These objectives basically make a guideline for all investment decisions. They cover several things such as an individual's current financial position, age and risk tolerance to future retirement plans, wealth accumulation or legacy goals. Every investor has unique circumstances that determine their investment strategy.

In this context, it is important to make a distinction between long-term and short-term investment strategies. In the case of long-term strategy, the usual approach is to remain invested in a diversified portfolio for several years. However, on the other hand, short term strategies are more about exploiting market inefficiencies within shorter durations. Both these strategies have advantages and disadvantages but they serve different investment purposes hence should be well understood before making any investment choices.

A crucial aspect of long-term investment strategies is patience and staying power. This kind of strategy often means investing in assets that will grow over time, despite market fluctuations in the short term. The objective here is to create wealth over a longer period at a gradual pace. Notable examples include Warren Buffet and Charlie Munger who are both proponents of "buy and hold".

On the flip side, short term investment strategies are focussed on quick profits made typically over just a few months or even days. Such strategies involve purchasing securities at low prices and selling them when their prices rise. This calls for expert knowledge in markets as it comes with significant risks due to volatility of markets within shorter periods.

In conclusion, whether to stay invested for long periods or trade frequently depends on an individual's personal financial goals, risk appetite as well as time horizon one has got to invest his money until maturity date reaches him/her.

## Understanding Investing Better

Risk however remains inherent in investments as we proceed further into investments however these can be managed by understanding them properly so that informed decision making may be done based on the set objectives Next up will be a detailed discussion on risk analysis and management which lays the foundation of a successful investing journey.

After risk assessment, risk management is necessary. The management of risk involves developing measures to reduce or control the identified risks. This can include spreading your investment across various asset classes, sectors or geographical locations; or putting a stop-loss order on trades to limit potential losses.

Risk management is designed not to eliminate all risks but manage them in line with investment objectives and risk appetite. For example, if you are building a portfolio for long-term goals like retirement and have a high tolerance for risk, you might choose to go aggressively and put most of your money into equities. On the other hand, if capital preservation is of utmost importance, you may want to be more cautious by investing mainly in bonds and other fixed income securities.

In finance as it currently stands, astute investors should make risk assessment and management their primary considerations in investment decisions. This will be an essential trait for a successful investment as global events keep changing bringing new challenges (and opportunities). The following part looks at ESG Investing - an emerging form of investment that does not only look at financial returns but also environmental, social and governance impacts.

## ESG Investing during Climate Change

Recently, there has been a trend among financiers to incorporate these issues into their investments through considering the environment, society and governance when making corporate decisions. Such type of investing is called ESG investing.

Environmental, Social and Governance (ESG) criteria refer to certain benchmarks used by ethical investors to evaluate how well a company operates. 'E' will consider how a company manages its impact on the environment. The 'S' refers to how the company interacts with employees, suppliers' customers' and communities where they operate while 'G' assesses the company's internal operations & leaderships while looking at shareholders rights as well as internal controls.

The growing emphasis on ESG investing reflects something larger happening within our society – our increasing awareness about choices that are sustainable for our planet. Consequently, ESG investing has started gaining momentum as Investors have realized the significance of supporting companies that have responsible business practices.

However, ESG investing goes beyond just making an impact on society but is also seen as a good risk management strategy. Consider climate change for example, A study by McKinsey & Company says that by 2030, climate change could impact up to $43 trillion of assets under management. Therefore, taking into account such factors like carbon footprint or fossil fuel exposure could help in mitigating losses that may arise due to climate-related risks.

For investors who want to generate long-term value creation, the scale and urgency of the climate crisis present new opportunities. Sustainable businesses may be better positioned in relation to regulatory shifts aimed at achieving net-zero emissions. They can also gain competitive advantage if they predict that customers will increasingly seek green products and services. Therefore, incorporating ESG criteria might give some insights on long-term adaptability and growth prospects for a corporation.

Furthermore, ESG investing is also not just about staying out of danger. It is about making the most of opportunities. In fact, those companies that are top performers in their industries as far as being environmentally responsible, socially aware and having good governance have a better chance of thriving in this modern-day world which is full of challenges, thereby showing superior financial performance and shareholder returns over time.

Nevertheless, ESG does provide extra insurance to investors while aligning your investments with your values and the kind of world you want to live in. Therefore, acknowledging financial instruments as drivers for change can allow us to make a difference towards a more inclusive and sustainable world as we move towards global sustainable development goals.

## Understanding Liquidity

In finance, liquidity refers to how easy it can be for an investor to buy or sell an asset or security without changing its price within the market. To put it simply, liquidity characterizes how quickly and easily a thing can be converted into cash. The asset's level of liquidity becomes very important for investors when they make decisions because it influences their ability to meet short-term financial obligations as well as capitalizing on market opportunities.

This sets the stage for understanding liquidity by looking at two broad categories: Liquidity Needs vs Illiquidity.

Liquidity Needs basically refers to how quickly an investor wants access to his or her money. For example, if one were putting aside money for retirement 30 years from now, they would not need a lot of liquidity unlike someone saving for a down payment on their next home within the next few years.

On the other hand we have illiquid assets that cannot be sold quickly without reducing significantly their price. Examples include private equity investments; real estate properties and various types of bonds among others. Conversely these illiquid investments often bear certain disadvantages whereas offering higher potential returns over the time span however disadvantageous are also inherent in them such as adverse prices resulting from forced selling and major losses.

Balancing between liquid and illiquid assets is essential to achieving financial success. Piling your portfolio with liquid assets only may result in you missing on some profitable investment alternatives that require longer term commitments. As well, having too many illiquid assets can leave you in need of cash at the time when least expected.

One way to maintain this balance is by investing in a Balanced Fund. This kind of mutual fund invests in a hybrid mixture of stocks and bonds. These funds are designed to provide for income, capital gains and conservative capital appreciation. The goal here is to allow for immediate liquidity while providing some exposure to higher return (but potentially riskier) assets.

You can create an effective investment strategy by considering your own liquidity needs and taking into account the illiquidity of certain investments. This will not only protect your short-term finances but also help you achieve long term investment goals.

**Setting Investment Goals**

To begin this journey towards financial freedom, it is important to first establish clear and attainable investment objectives. The first key step in developing a successful investment strategy involves understanding what one wants to accomplish through his or her investments. Many objectives can be made for investments like saving for a vacation or a car. They can also be long-term goals such as retirement plans or education plans for your children. Your investment portfolio should reflect those goals so that your specific needs should be met in terms of returns and risk profile.

Remember also that achieving financial returns is not just about making the most money possible. It means that you have been able to meet your financial targets within the time limits while considering factors such as risk tolerance, liquidity needs and asset class suitability.Particularly,suitability entails how appropriate an investment product or strategy is with respect to one's financial situation,risk profile and objectives.Equity mutual funds might be suitable if you have a 20-year investment horizon and have moderate risk-tolerance, for instance.

An important part of setting goals is understanding Risk management approach. It is an analytical process that helps us identify and manage potential risks associated with an investment decision. This incorporates various techniques which seek to cushion unpredictable events from impacting negatively on the value of your portfolio.

Diversification across sectors or geographies, managing volatility through hedging strategies, constant monitoring of market trends for possible threats, and maintaining adequate cash reserves during bad economic times are some elements of an efficient risk management approach. This may also include mitigation investments which provide a cushion against losses in case other investments do not perform well.

Moreover, behavioral finance has a role in setting investment goals. Behavioral finance represents psychology-based theories that explain market anomalies. Rather than our investing decisions being rational all the time they are often driven by emotions and cognitive errors. These biases once identified can assist in coming up with logical choices concerning investments; loss aversion bias, for example, avoids loses more than it seeks equivalent gains thereby preventing hasty decisions when there is a drop in the stock market.

Finally,it's essential to review investment goals periodically. The performance of your investments should be monitored against your objectives and adjustments made along the way as necessary. It may involve rebalancing your portfolio or revising your financial plans due to changes in your personal circumstances or financial markets.

It is not something you come across once and forget when setting investment goals. It is a continuing dialogue with yourself about what you want out of life and how your finances can help you achieve that. With clear investment objectives at the helm, every decision made on a daily basis will be guided towards long-term financial success.

# Chapter 2

# Venture Capital 101

Venture capital is a crucial source of funding for new, growing, or troubled businesses. It involves an outside investor providing financial support to a business in exchange for an equity stake. Venture capital funds are organized as limited partnerships or open-ended corporate structures. Managers of these funds typically earn a fixed annual fee of 2% of invested capital, along with a "Carried Interest" of 20% of the fund's income. This income consists of long-term capital gains and qualified dividends taxed at 15%.

Key Takeaways:

- Venture capital is funding provided by an outside investor in exchange for equity.
- VC funds are typically structured as limited partnerships or open-ended corporate structures.
- Fund managers earn a fixed annual fee and a "Carried Interest" based on the fund's income.
- The income received by venture capitalists includes long-term capital gains and qualified dividends.
- VC is a vital source of funding for new, growing, and troubled businesses.

**Private Funds and Accredited Investors**

Venture capital funds offer private funds to investors through "Private Transactions" that do not involve a public offering. These private transactions are exempt from registration under the Securities Act of 1933. However, to qualify for these exemptions, the offering must be limited to a small number of financially sophisticated investors who are known as Accredited "Reg. D Investors."

Regulation D, a provision under the 1933 Act, provides a regulatory safe harbor for venture capital funds when offering Limited Partnership interests. VC funds carefully limit the number and types of investors who can participate in the fund based on certain criteria, such as net worth or annual income.

| Private Funds | Accredited Investors | Regulation D |
|---|---|---|
| Private transactions exempt from registration | Small number of financially sophisticated investors | Regulatory safe harbor for Limited Partnership interests |
| Limited to qualified investors | Criteria based on net worth or annual income | Ensures compliance with securities regulations |

**Carried Interest Misconception and Reality**

Carried interest is an agreement among partners to allow venture capitalists (VC) to share in the partnership's profit. VC earn carried interest as compensation for adding value and working side-by-side with entrepreneurs.

Limited partners want VCs to receive carry reward only in the long-term when a company exit brings economic value to the team—entrepreneurs, investors, and VCs.

The structure of VC funds allows for capital calls to advance more capital as investments are made, and funds are distributed back to limited partners after exits, less the carry and expenses.

**The J-Curve Effect and Mitigating Strategies**

The J-Curve effect is a phenomenon commonly observed in venture capital investments. It refers to the declining net cash flow experienced in the early years of a venture capital fund before gradually increasing and eventually turning positive.

Venture capitalists are known for seeking higher returns, which often requires taking on higher-risk investments. As a result, they cannot afford to focus solely on low- to medium-risk opportunities.

To mitigate the effects of the J-Curve and decrease volatility, venture capital funds employ various strategies. One common approach is to make steady, annual commitments to create a disciplined investment strategy. This helps distribute the investment risk evenly over time and smoothens the cash flow fluctuations.

Another significant mitigating strategy is creating a well-diversified portfolio of investment exits. By spreading investments across multiple companies with different stages of growth, industries, and geographical locations, funds can reduce the impact of any single investment underperforming.

Overall, mitigating the J-Curve effect requires careful planning, disciplined investment strategies, and portfolio diversification. By implementing these strategies, venture capital funds aim to minimize risk and optimize returns for their investors.

## Venture Capital Firms

Venture capital firms (VCs) play a crucial role in fueling the growth and innovation of startups. These firms raise capital from a variety of sources, including family offices, institutional investors, and high net worth individuals, to invest in promising entrepreneurial ventures. By providing funding, expertise, and valuable connections, venture capital firms help startups navigate the challenging early stages of their business journey.

VCs act as money management organizations, carefully selecting and investing the collective capital they have raised into startups that show the potential for significant growth and profitability. The size of VC investments can vary depending on the specific investment theory and practices of each firm.

What sets venture capital firms apart is their ability to provide more than just funding. They often specialize in supporting startups in specific stages, industries, or geographic regions, bringing industry knowledge and mentorship to the table. This specialization allows VCs to provide strategic advice and guidance tailored to the unique needs of the startups they invest in, increasing their chances of success.

Additionally, venture capital firms play a vital role in the overall economy by fostering innovation, creating jobs, and driving economic growth. They bridge the gap between promising but risky startups and traditional funding sources such as banks, allowing entrepreneurs to access the capital they need to bring their ideas to life.

Benefits of Venture Capital Firms:

- *Access to Capital:* Venture capital firms provide startups with the funding they need to grow and scale their operations.
- *Expertise and Support:* VCs offer strategic guidance, industry knowledge, and valuable connections that can help startups overcome challenges and achieve their goals.
- *Mentorship and Networks:* Venture capital firms often have extensive networks of entrepreneurs, industry experts, and potential customers, which can help startups access valuable resources and opportunities.
- *Long-Term Partnership:* Unlike other sources of funding, venture capital firms typically take a long-term approach and are committed to supporting startups throughout their growth journey.

| Venture Capital Firm | Specialization | Investment Focus |
|---|---|---|
| XYZ Venture Partners | Healthcare | Early-stage technology startups in the healthcare sector |
| ABC Capital | Software | Mid-stage software companies with a focus on artificial intelligence |
| 123 Ventures | Clean Energy | Late-stage clean energy companies with proven technologies |

**Venture Capital Funds and Limited Partners**

Venture capital funds play a crucial role in financing innovative startups and fueling their growth. These funds are created by pooling money from various investors, known as limited partners (LPs). LPs can include institutional investors, high net worth individuals, and family offices seeking to diversify their investment portfolios and tap into the potential of high-growth companies.

The objective of LPs in investing in venture capital funds is to achieve a certain overall percentage of return each year. By allocating a portion of their capital to these funds, LPs can potentially benefit from the high-risk, high-reward nature of venture capital investments. This allows them to participate in the success of promising startups and unlock significant returns on their investment over time.

To efficiently manage these funds, venture capital firms appoint general partners (GPs) who make investment decisions and oversee the fund's operations. The GPs act as the bridge between the LPs and the portfolio companies, ensuring that the funds are invested strategically to maximize returns while aligning with the investment objectives of the LPs.

By leveraging the expertise and resources of the venture capital firm, LPs can access a diversified portfolio of startup investments that they might not have been able to identify or evaluate individually. This partnership model allows LPs to benefit from the active involvement of experienced professionals in the investment process, enhancing the chances of success.

**Fund Managers and Returns**

Fund managers, also known as general partners (GPs), play a crucial role in venture capital by investing capital in high-potential startups and delivering returns to the limited partners (LPs) who have invested in the fund. GPs are responsible for making strategic investment decisions, managing the portfolio of investments, and actively supporting the growth of the companies in which they invest.

Along with their expertise, fund managers typically charge management fees and carried interest on the profits generated from the fund's investments. Management fees are a fixed percentage of the fund's assets and cover the operating expenses of the fund, including salaries, office rent, and other administrative costs. Carried interest, on the other hand, is a share of the profits made on the fund's investments. It acts as an incentive for fund managers to deliver strong returns.

When it comes to returns on investment in venture capital, the landscape follows a power law distribution. This means that a small number of top-performing VC funds generate a significant majority of the returns, while the majority of funds produce more modest returns. The power law distribution highlights the importance of selecting the right fund managers and investing in funds that have a proven track record of success.

*"The power law distribution in venture capital means that the difference in returns between top-performing funds and the rest is significant. It's crucial for investors to carefully evaluate the performance and track record of fund managers before committing capital."*

**Comparing Returns of Top-Performing VC Funds and Rest of the Funds**

| Category | Average Returns on Investment |
|---|---|
| Top-Performing VC Funds | 20-30% annualized returns |
| Rest of the Funds | 5-10% annualized returns |

As shown in the table above, the top-performing VC funds consistently deliver higher returns, typically ranging from 20-30% annualized. These funds have a proven ability to identify and invest in successful startups, resulting in significant financial gains for their investors.

Conversely, the rest of the funds, which comprise the majority, tend to generate more modest returns, ranging from 5-10% annualized. These funds may still contribute to a diversified investment portfolio, providing stability and potential upside, but their returns are generally lower.

Investors seeking to maximize their returns on venture capital investments should consider allocating a portion of their portfolio to top-performing funds. By doing so, they can capitalize on the power law distribution and increase their chances of achieving significant long-term gains.

## Venture Capital Funding Process

The process of securing venture capital funding involves several key steps, starting with the submission of a comprehensive business plan to venture capitalists (VCs). This initial stage is crucial, as it serves as the first introduction to the business and its potential for growth and success. The business plan should provide a clear overview of the company's market opportunity, competitive advantage, financial projections, and growth strategy.

Once the business plan has been submitted, the next step is to engage in introductory conversations and meetings with the VCs. These discussions are aimed at assessing the mutual fit between the business and the VC firm. It is essential for both parties to align in terms of goals, values, and expectations.

If there is interest from the VCs after the initial meetings, the due diligence process begins. Due diligence is a comprehensive evaluation of the business, its market, and its management team. It involves analyzing the market opportunity, assessing the growth potential, conducting interviews with key executives, and evaluating the business strategy.

*"Due diligence is a critical phase as it allows VCs to gain a deeper understanding of the business and its potential for success. It is a way to validate the claims made in the business plan and ensure that the investment aligns with the VC's investment criteria and portfolio strategy."*

If the due diligence phase is satisfactory and the VC firm believes in the potential of the business, they will typically offer a term sheet. A term sheet outlines the key terms and conditions of the investment, including the amount of funding, the valuation of the company, and the rights and obligations of both parties.

Once the term sheet is agreed upon, the next step is the legal documentation. This involves drafting and reviewing legal agreements, such as the investment agreement, shareholder agreement, and any other necessary contracts. It is essential to seek legal advice during this process to ensure that all parties are protected and that the terms of the investment are properly documented.

Finally, once the legal documentation is complete and all parties are satisfied, the funds are made available to the business. This capital infusion enables the company to execute its growth plans, expand its operations, and achieve its milestones.

## Venture Capital Funding Process Overview

| Step | Description |
|------|-------------|
| 1. Business Plan Submission | Submit a comprehensive business plan to VCs. |
| 2. Introductory Conversations | Engage in discussions to assess mutual fit. |
| 3. Due Diligence | Evaluate the business, market, and management team. |
| 4. Term Sheet | Offer and agree upon the key terms and conditions. |
| 5. Legal Documentation | Draft and review legal agreements. |
| 6. Funds Availability | Make the capital available to the business. |

## Types of Venture Capital Funding

In the world of venture capital, funding is categorized into different rounds, each serving a specific purpose in the growth journey of a startup. Understanding these funding rounds is crucial for entrepreneurs seeking capital to fuel their ventures. Let's explore the various types of venture capital funding:

### 1. Seed Capital:

Seed capital is the initial funding provided to early-stage startups. It helps entrepreneurs turn their ideas into viable businesses. Seed capital is often obtained from angel investors, friends and family, or early-stage venture capital firms. This funding is used to conduct market research, develop a prototype, build a team, and validate the business concept.

### 2. Startup Capital:

Once a startup has a viable product or service and is ready to enter the market, it may seek startup capital. This funding is used to support the initial commercialization efforts of the business. It helps in scaling operations, refining the product, establishing a customer base, and covering early marketing expenses.

### 3. Series A, B, C, and D Rounds:

As a startup progresses and achieves significant milestones, it may require additional funding for expansion and growth. Series A, B, C, and D rounds represent the successive rounds of financing a startup can secure as it advances through different stages of growth. Each round typically involves larger investments than the previous one and is provided by venture capital firms, institutional investors, or corporate venture arms.

"Venture capital funding is categorized into various rounds, such as seed capital for early-stage ventures, startup capital for companies with a sample product, and series A, B, C, and D rounds for middle and later-stage funding."

### 4. Mezzanine Round:

The mezzanine round bridges the gap between late-stage venture capital funding and an IPO (Initial Public Offering) or acquisition. This funding helps startups prepare for the next phase of growth, such as expanding market reach, optimizing operations, or preparing for liquidity events.

### 5. Late-Stage and Pre-IPO Funding:

When a startup is nearing an IPO or acquisition, it may require significant capital to fuel its final growth push. Late-stage financing and pre-IPO funding provide the necessary capital to support substantial expansion, strategic acquisitions, or other business initiatives aimed at achieving the desired valuation or liquidity event.

In summary, venture capital funding encompasses seed capital, startup capital, series A, B, C, and D rounds, mezzanine financing, late-stage funding, and pre-IPO funding. Each funding round caters to different stages of a startup's growth, and securing the right type of funding at each stage is vital for success.

| Funding Round | Description |
| --- | --- |
| Seed Capital | Initial funding for early-stage startups |
| Startup Capital | Funding to support the initial commercialization efforts |
| Series A, B, C, and D Rounds | Successive rounds of financing as a startup progresses |
| Mezzanine Round | Funding between late-stage VC and IPO/acquisition |
| Late-Stage and Pre-IPO Funding | Funding for final growth push before going public or being acquired |

**Alternatives to Venture Capital**

While venture capital can be a valuable source of funding for businesses, it is not the only option available. In fact, there are alternative financing routes that entrepreneurs can explore to meet their funding needs. Two popular alternatives are angel investors and strategic investors.

Angel investors are individuals who provide capital to early-stage businesses in exchange for equity. Unlike venture capital firms, angel investors typically invest smaller amounts of money and are often willing to take on more risk. However, they also offer valuable guidance and mentorship based on their own entrepreneurial experiences.

On the other hand, strategic investors are companies or individuals who invest in businesses for specific reasons beyond financial returns. These investors may have a particular interest in a company's technology, products, or market presence. Strategic investors often have deeper pockets, allowing them to make larger investments. In addition to capital, they may bring partnerships, licensing agreements, or other strategic advantages to the table.

When considering alternatives to venture capital, it is crucial for entrepreneurs to assess their specific needs and goals. Angel investors can be a great fit for early-stage startups seeking guidance and moderate funding, while strategic investors can provide the necessary capital and valuable partnerships for companies with unique technologies or market opportunities. By aligning their funding sources with their business requirements, entrepreneurs can set themselves up for success.

# Angels Among Us

Welcome to chapter 3 of our series on startup funding. In this chapter, we will explore the world of angel investors and their impact on early-stage startups. Angel investors are key players in fostering innovation and driving economic growth.

Let's dive into the fascinating realm of angel investing and discover how these investors support and propel the entrepreneurial ecosystem.

## Who Are Angel Investors?

"Angel investors are the lifeblood of early-stage startups, providing crucial funding and support for entrepreneurs. These individuals, often high net worth individuals, play a vital role in fueling innovation and driving economic growth in the startup ecosystem. In addition to financial backing, angel investors bring valuable industry experience and mentorship to the table, helping startups navigate the challenges of building a successful business."

"Unlike venture capitalists who manage funds from other investors, angel investors typically invest their own money in exchange for equity or ownership in the startup. This personal investment often demonstrates a genuine belief in the potential of the startup and a commitment to its success. Angel investors are not just passive investors; they actively participate in the growth and development of the startups they support, offering guidance, mentorship, and valuable connections."

"The role of angel investors goes beyond funding; they are often seen as mentors and trusted advisors. Their industry expertise and network can be invaluable to startups, especially those in their early stages. From providing strategic advice to making introductions to potential partners or customers, angel investors bring a wealth of knowledge and resources to the startups they support."

## The Importance of Angel Investing in Early-Stage Startups

Angel investing plays a vital role in the success of early-stage startups, providing the necessary capital to fuel their growth and development. This form of funding allows entrepreneurs to transform their innovative ideas into thriving businesses, catapulting them towards success and economic prosperity.

*"Angel investing is like giving oxygen to a spark, igniting the flames of innovation and propelling startups towards their full potential."*

Without angel investors, many aspiring entrepreneurs would struggle to secure the funding needed to bring their ideas to life. Traditional sources of funding, such as bank loans, may be difficult to obtain for startups due to limited collateral or a lack of financial history. Angel investing fills this gap by providing a critical injection of funds, enabling startups to hire talent, develop products, and execute marketing strategies to drive growth.

Angel investors are not just passive sources of funding; they often take an active role in guiding and mentoring startups. Their extensive industry experience and networks can provide invaluable insights and connections that help startups navigate the complexities of business operations and market challenges.

Moreover, angel investors contribute to the overall growth of the startup ecosystem. By supporting early-stage startups, they foster a culture of innovation and entrepreneurship that fuels economic development and job creation. The ripple effect of successful startups can be felt across industries, driving technological advancements and disrupting traditional business models.

In summary, angel investing is not only about funding; it is about fostering the growth and development of early-stage startups. It is about empowering entrepreneurs to turn their visions into reality and driving innovation that propels our society forward.

| Benefits of Angel Investing | Risks and Considerations | Real World Examples |
|---|---|---|
| 1. Capital for growth | 1. Market volatility | 1. Peter Thiel - early investor in Facebook |
| 2. Mentorship and guidance | 2. Early-stage startups' high failure rate | 2. Ashton Kutcher - invested in Airbnb and Uber |
| 3. Industry expertise | 3. Lack of liquidity | 3. Chris Sacca - invested in Twitter and Instagram |

## Differences Between Angel Investors and Venture Capitalists

When it comes to funding early-stage startups, angel investors and venture capitalists play crucial roles. While both provide financial support to entrepreneurs, there are distinct differences between these two types of investors.

*Angel investors* are typically high net worth individuals who invest their own money in startups. They often have a personal interest in the success of the company and take a hands-on approach to their investments. Angel investors tend to make smaller investments compared to venture capitalists, with an average investment size ranging from $25,000 to $100,000. They see themselves as mentors and advisors, offering guidance and industry expertise to the entrepreneurs they back.

*Venture capitalists*, on the other hand, manage funds from other investors and invest in startups on behalf of those funds. They typically have larger investment sizes, ranging from a few hundred thousand dollars to several million dollars. Venture capitalists have a more formalized investment process and often take a more passive role in the companies they invest in.

*"Angel investors are like your cool aunt or uncle who believes in your dreams and supports you every step of the way, while venture capitalists are more like institutional investors who bet on promising startups but don't get involved in the day-to-day operations."*

The level of involvement is another key difference between angel investors and venture capitalists. Angel investors are known for their hands-on approach, providing mentorship and support to the entrepreneurs they invest in. They bring valuable industry connections and expertise to the table, helping startups navigate the challenges of building a successful business. Venture capitalists, on the other hand, tend to take a more hands-off approach. They often have larger portfolios and may not have the time or resources to provide the same level of individualized support as angel investors. However, venture capitalists can offer access to a wider network of contacts and resources, which can be beneficial to startups.

Overall, both angel investors and venture capitalists play crucial roles in the startup ecosystem. While angel investors provide early-stage funding and personalized support, venture capitalists bring larger investment sizes and a broader network of contacts. Understanding the differences between these two types of investors can help entrepreneurs determine the best funding sources for their startups.

## Real World Examples of Angel Investors

Angel investors have played a pivotal role in the success of numerous startups, providing essential funding and guidance to help these ventures thrive. Let's take a look at some notable angel investors who have made significant contributions to the startup ecosystem.

## Peter Thiel

*"Competition is for losers."*

Peter Thiel, co-founder of PayPal and Palantir, is widely regarded as one of the most influential angel investors in the tech industry. Thiel's early investment in Facebook in 2004 was a game-changer, contributing to the social media giant's growth and success. Thiel's focus on disruptive and innovative startups has made him a prominent figure in the angel investing community.

**Ashton Kutcher**

*"Opportunities look like work."*

Aside from his successful acting career, Ashton Kutcher has also made a name for himself as an angel investor. His investments in companies like Airbnb and Uber have not only generated substantial returns but have also helped fuel the growth of these industry disruptors. Kutcher's passion for technology and startups has made him a respected figure in the angel investing world.

**Shervin Pishevar**

*"An entrepreneur is someone who dreams big and is willing to work hard to make those dreams come true."*

Shervin Pishevar is an Iranian-American entrepreneur and angel investor who has made significant contributions to the startup ecosystem. As the founder of Sherpa Capital, Pishevar has invested in numerous successful companies, including Airbnb, Uber, and Slack. His ability to identify promising startups and provide valuable mentorship has made him a sought-after angel investor.

**Guy Kawasaki**

*"Get going. Get started. Iterate. Iterate. Iterate. Only great teams with a great product can achieve greatness."*

Guy Kawasaki, a renowned venture capitalist and former Apple employee, is known for his expertise in angel investing. He has invested in a wide range of startups, offering his extensive industry knowledge and experience to help them succeed.

Kawasaki's impact in the startup world extends beyond his investments, as he also works as a speaker, author, and evangelist for entrepreneurship.

| Name | Notable Investments |
| --- | --- |
| Peter Thiel | Facebook, SpaceX, Airbnb |
| Ashton Kutcher | Airbnb, Uber, Spotify |
| Shervin Pishevar | Uber, Airbnb, Slack |
| Guy Kawasaki | Canva, Ring, Medium |

**Benefits of Angel Investors for Startups**

Working with angel investors can provide numerous advantages for startups, ranging from financial support to valuable industry expertise and connections. These benefits are instrumental in helping startups overcome challenges and achieve success.

**1. Funding Support:**

One of the primary benefits of angel investors is their ability to provide funding for startups. Unlike traditional loans, angel investments involve equity financing, allowing startups to access capital without incurring debt. This funding can be critical for covering operational expenses, product development, marketing efforts, and scaling the business.

**2. Industry Expertise:**

Angel investors often bring extensive industry experience and knowledge to the table, which can be immensely valuable for startups. Their expertise allows them to provide strategic guidance, mentorship, and insights into market trends, helping startups navigate challenges and make informed decisions.

**3. Business Network:**

Angel investors typically have robust professional networks, which can open doors for startups. Through their connections, startups gain access to potential customers, partners, and suppliers.

This network can significantly enhance the startup's market reach, create partnership opportunities, and increase the chances of success.

## 4. Mentorship and Guidance:

Unlike traditional investors, angel investors often take a more hands-on approach and offer mentorship to startups. They provide guidance and support based on their own entrepreneurial journeys, helping founders avoid common pitfalls and capitalize on opportunities. Their mentorship can accelerate the learning curve and foster the growth of startups.

## 5. Validation and Credibility:

Securing investment from reputable angel investors can lend credibility to startups. The endorsement of experienced investors acts as a stamp of approval, making it easier for startups to attract additional funding, customers, and strategic partnerships. This validation enhances the startup's reputation and increases its chances of long-term success.

| Benefits of Angel Investors for Startups | Description |
|---|---|
| Funding Support | Provides capital without incurring debt |
| Industry Expertise | Brings valuable knowledge and guidance |
| Business Network | Access to potential customers, partners, and suppliers |
| Mentorship and Guidance | Offers support and advice based on experience |
| Validation and Credibility | Enhances reputation and attracts additional opportunities |

## How to Attract Angel Investors

Attracting angel investors is a crucial step for startups looking to secure funding and propel their growth. To catch the attention of these potential backers, entrepreneurs need to employ effective strategies that highlight their unique value proposition and growth potential.

## The Compelling Pitch Deck

A well-crafted pitch deck is a powerful tool for attracting angel investors. It should concisely present the startup's mission, target market, competitive advantage, and financial projections. The pitch deck should emphasize the potential return on investment for angel investors while clearly explaining how their funds will be utilized to achieve milestones and foster growth.

Building a Network and Establishing Relationships

In the startup ecosystem, networking plays a vital role in connecting with angel investors. Attending industry events, startup conferences, and networking sessions can provide invaluable opportunities to meet potential investors. Establishing relationships with mentors, advisors, and fellow entrepreneurs can also lead to introductions to angel investors who may be interested in the startup's industry or niche.

## Demonstrating Traction and Progress

Angel investors are attracted to startups that have demonstrated traction and progress. Providing evidence of customer acquisition, revenue growth, or product development milestones can significantly enhance the startup's appeal. Startups should showcase their ability to execute their business plan, validate their market potential, and capitalize on opportunities in their industry.

By following these strategies and presenting a compelling pitch deck, entrepreneurs can increase their chances of attracting angel investors who are enthusiastic about their innovative ideas and are willing to provide the necessary support and funding for their startup's success.

Risks and Considerations for Angel Investors

Angel investing can be a rewarding endeavor for investors looking to support innovative startups and potentially reap significant financial returns. However, it's important to recognize and assess the risks associated with angel investments. Conducting thorough due diligence is crucial for making informed investment decisions and minimizing potential pitfalls.

When considering angel investments, factors such as market conditions, competition, and the strength of the founding team should be carefully evaluated. Let's take a closer look at some key risks and considerations for angel investors:

## Evaluating Market Conditions

Understanding the market in which a startup operates is essential for assessing its growth potential. Market conditions can fluctuate, and investors need to determine if there is sufficient demand for the product or service offered by the startup. Conducting market research and analyzing industry trends can provide valuable insights into the market's size, competition, and potential risks.

## Assessing Competition

A startup's ability to differentiate itself from competitors is crucial for long-term success. Investors should assess the competitive landscape and evaluate the startup's unique value proposition. Understanding the competitive advantages a startup has, such as patented technology, a strong brand, or strategic partnerships, can help investors gauge its potential for sustainable growth.

## Evaluating the Founding Team

The strength and experience of a startup's founding team can greatly impact its chances of success. Angel investors should evaluate the team's expertise, track record, and their ability to execute the business plan. A cohesive and capable team with a strong vision and complementary skill sets increases the likelihood of overcoming challenges and achieving milestones.

## Financial Considerations

Investing in startups involves a level of financial risk, as there is no guarantee of returns. Angel investors should carefully consider the financial implications of their investments and assess the startup's financial projections and burn rate. It's important to have a clear understanding of the potential return on investment and the timeline for achieving profitability or attracting additional funding.

## Conducting Due Diligence

Thorough due diligence is crucial for angel investors to mitigate risks and make informed investment decisions. This process involves investigating the startup's financial health, legal compliance, intellectual property rights, and potential risks. It may also include conducting background checks on the founding team and seeking expert advice to validate the startup's claims and projections.

*"Angel investing comes with inherent risks, and it's important for investors to conduct thorough due diligence before making investment decisions."*

By carefully assessing these risks and conducting due diligence, angel investors can make informed investment decisions and increase their chances of supporting successful startups. While there is always inherent risk involved, taking a thoughtful approach can help mitigate potential pitfalls and maximize the opportunities for both investors and entrepreneurs.

| Risks | Considerations |
|---|---|
| Market conditions | Evaluate growth potential, demand, and industry trends |
| Competition | Assess the startup's unique value proposition and competitive advantages |
| Founding team | Evaluate expertise, track record, and ability to execute |
| Financial considerations | Assess financial projections, ROI, and potential for profitability |
| Due diligence | Conduct thorough investigation, validate claims, seek expert advice |

**Angel Investor Networks and Platforms**

Startups looking for angel investors to fund their ventures and investors seeking promising investment opportunities can leverage various angel investor networks and platforms. These platforms serve as a bridge between entrepreneurs and investors, facilitating connections and fostering collaboration.

*"Angel investor networks and platforms provide an invaluable resource for startups to showcase their businesses and attract potential investors. They offer a streamlined process for entrepreneurs to access angel investor communities and increase their chances of securing funding."*

Angel investor networks bring together a community of like-minded individuals who have a shared interest in investing in early-stage startups. These networks actively connect startups with angel investors who have a keen eye for promising investment opportunities.

On the other hand, platforms designed specifically for angel investors provide a centralized hub for finding investment opportunities. These platforms allow investors to browse through a curated selection of startups, review their pitch decks, and make informed investment decisions.

**Benefits of Angel Investor Networks and Platforms**

Angel investor networks and platforms offer several advantages for both startups and investors:

| Benefits for Startups | Benefits for Investors |
| --- | --- |
| Increased visibility and exposure to a wide network of angel investors | Access to a diverse pool of promising startups |
| Mentorship and guidance from experienced angel investors | Opportunity to diversify investment portfolios |
| Potential for syndicate investments that pool resources from multiple investors | Easier access to due diligence materials and startup information |

In addition to connecting startups with investors, some angel investor networks and platforms also offer additional resources such as educational materials, networking events, and pitching competitions, further enhancing the startup ecosystem.

**Trends in Angel Investing**

The landscape of angel investing is constantly evolving, reflecting the changing priorities and motivations of angel investors. Several notable trends have emerged in the world of angel investing, including:

**Impact Investing**

Impact investing focuses on funding startups that generate positive social or environmental impact, along with financial returns. Angel investors are increasingly recognizing the power of their investments to make a difference and are actively seeking opportunities to support companies that align with their values.

**Supporting Diverse Founders**

There is a growing emphasis on supporting and funding startups founded by underrepresented entrepreneurs, such as women, minorities, and individuals from marginalized communities. Angel investors understand the importance of diversity in driving innovation and are actively seeking out diverse founders to invest in.

"Supporting a diverse range of founders not only fosters innovation but also creates a more inclusive entrepreneurial ecosystem."

**Investing in Social Entrepreneurship**

Social entrepreneurship refers to the practice of using business strategies to address social and environmental challenges. Angel investors are increasingly drawn to startups that have a clear mission to create a positive impact in society, alongside sustainable financial growth.

Angel investing is not just about financial returns anymore. It is driven by a desire for meaningful impact and change in society. These trends highlight the commitment of angel investors to support startups that align with their values and contribute positively to the world.

**The Impact of Angel Investors on Innovation**

Angel investors play a crucial role in driving innovation and fostering economic growth within the startup ecosystem. Their financial backing provides much-needed capital for early-stage startups, allowing them to turn their groundbreaking ideas into reality. In addition to their financial contributions, angel investors bring valuable mentorship and industry expertise to the table, helping startups navigate the challenges of building a successful business.

By supporting startups in their early stages, angel investors contribute to the overall growth and development of the entrepreneurial landscape. They provide the necessary resources for startups to experiment, iterate, and refine their innovative solutions, pushing the boundaries of what is possible. Through their involvement, angel investors not only fuel the individual success of startups but also contribute to the collective progress of various industries.

The impact of angel investors on innovation extends beyond individual startups. By investing in promising ventures and encouraging entrepreneurship, they create a ripple effect that leads to job creation, economic stimulation, and technological advancements. The success of angel-backed startups inspires other entrepreneurs, fosters a culture of innovation, and attracts further investment, creating a positive feedback loop that drives economic growth at a broader scale.

# Chapter 4

# The Art of Valuation

When attempting to establish or scale a business, especially a startup or growth-stage venture, understanding the concept and intricacies of valuation becomes critical.

Valuation is not just about putting a price tag on your company, but it's also an essential procedure that gives you insights into where your business stands in the market.

With proper valuation, you gain access to potential funding opportunities, strategic partnerships, and exit strategies. More significantly for startups and growth-stage businesses, valuation sets the stage for future fundraising rounds.

## Valuing Startup Ventures

The process of valuing startup ventures differs substantially from established ones. Traditional methods of valuation fall short when applied to startups due to their unique nature and business dynamics. They lack the historical financial data that most valuation models require and have a higher risk profile compared to mature firms. Valuation in this realm requires a degree of art mixed with science, guided by industry experience and market trends.

According to a "Startup Valuation Guide", many factors affect startup valuation, including the strength of the management team, market size, intellectual property, and competitive environment. However, one must also note that every investor will weigh these elements differently based on their investment philosophy and risk tolerance.

## Growth-Stage Business Valuation

Valuation for growth-stage businesses is a different ball game altogether. After surpassing the uncertainties of the startup phase, these companies have more substantial operational history under their belt. They are now focused on scaling their operations and expanding their market reach. Hence, unlike startups, growth-stage businesses can be valued using traditional methods with slight modifications.

A "valuation of growth-stage businesses" report suggests considering key metrics such as monthly recurring revenue (MRR), customer acquisition cost (CAC), lifetime value of a customer (LTV), churn rate, and gross margin. These key indicators reveal the company's health and the effectiveness of its business model.

In conclusion, understanding the art and science of valuation is essential for startups and growth-stage businesses to capture their actual value and leverage it for future growth and investor relationships. As we navigate through the book, we'll delve deeper into different traditional and modern methods applied in startup and growth-stage business valuations, implications of market trends on valuation, common misunderstandings and mistakes, as well as best practices to get your startup or growth-stage business valuation right.

## Valuation Methods for Startups and Growth-Stage Businesses

Several methods exist to determine the valuation of a startup or growth-stage business, each offering its unique perspective and insights. While some focus on the business's future potential, others look at current financial performance or market position.

The most commonly used startup valuation methods are the Discounted Cash Flow (DCF) Analysis, Market Method, Income Approach and Earnings Multiplier method.

## Discounted Cash Flow (DCF) Analysis

The Discounted Cash Flow analysis is a detailed financial model that uses projected cash flows to calculate your company's present value. While it can be complex to prepare initially, it's one of the most accurate methods since it primarily focuses on tangible financial data. The more accurate your projections, the more reliable your valuation will be.

## Market Method

The Market Method evaluates comparable publicly traded companies and recent acquisition transactions within your industry. It provides an understanding of how similar businesses are valued in the marketplace. However, finding perfect comparable in the case of startups can be challenging due to their unique business dynamics and often disruptive nature.

## Income Approach

The Income approach involves valuing a company based on its ability to generate economic benefit for its owners. The method converts anticipated economic benefits into a present single amount adjusting for risk and time value of money. The usefulness of this method is limited if your startup is pre-revenue or if its income is highly unpredictable.

## Earnings Multiplier

In an Earnings Multiplier approach, valuation is determined by multiplying profit or earnings by an industry-specific multiplier formula often derived from observing past transactions. This method may not always be the best fit for early startups as they might not have consistent revenue or earnings.

While these are some of the conventional ways to determine startup valuation, developing a comprehensive understanding of these models is critical before application. Each startup's situation and context may dictate a different approach. Furthermore, even though these methods are widely accepted, they can still lead to vastly differing valuations – an aspect that often leads to contentious debates amongst founders and investors.

In addition to these, there are other more modern approaches like 'Risk Factor Summation' and 'Berkus Method', which take into account the many risks associated with startups. It's essential to understand that no single method is foolproof or accurate in all scenarios. Mix and match your strategies according to your company's characteristics to get the most realistic valuation.

## The Impact of Market Trends on Startup Valuation

It often goes unnoticed, but market trends and circumstances play a significant role in determining a startup or growth-stage business's valuation. Although the primary focus is on financials and operational metrics, external factors such as economic climate, industry advances, competition, and investor sentiment cannot be overlooked as they shape the business landscape dramatically.

## Economic Climate

The economic state plays an indispensable role in shaping investor expectations and determining your company's value. During a booming economy, optimistic expectations lead to higher valuations because investors believe that startups have a better chance of growing quickly. Conversely, in a downturn, valuations often decrease due to leaner times ahead.

## Industry Trends

Innovation can rapidly shift established markets — just consider how streaming services disrupted the traditional cable TV industry. A bright idea with strong execution capabilities can yield exponential growth for startups in trendy sectors. Rapid advancements in artificial intelligence (AI), machine learning, blockchain technology, and health tech recently have elevated the valuation multiples for startups operating within these fields.

## Competition and Market Saturation

Intense competition can directly impact a startup's valuation. While competition validates market demand and could be seen as positive signs by some investors, too much of it could signal potential future roadblocks in gaining market share. Therefore, it's vital to understand the competitive dynamics within your specific marketplace during the valuation process.

Investor Sentiment

The mood of venture capitalists and other investors can sway startup valuations significantly. If there's an abundance of capital chasing limited opportunities or if there are high-return success stories from recent IPOs or acquisitions, investors may be willing to pay more than usual leading to 'hot money' investing, driving up valuations.

However, be wary of inflated valuations due to over-optimistic market sentiment. These could lead to a subsequent 'down round,' which might dilute your ownership stake and harm your company's reputation among future investors.

To encapsulate, while internal factors and methodologies remain critical, understanding the market conditions and their implications on your startup's valuation is pivotal. While it's not possible to control these external factors, being aware of them can help you strategically navigate the fundraising process, communicate effectively with prospective investors and adopt proactive measures to protect your business.

## Common Mistakes in Startup Valuation

Startup valuation is a complex process with an array of variables to be taken into account. In this challenging process, it's common for entrepreneurs and investors alike to fall prey to certain misconceptions and errors that can lead to incorrect valuations, causing severe implications at later stages. Thus, it's critical to understand and avoid these pitfalls when determining your startup's worth.

## Overestimating Future Financial Projections

One of the most common mistakes in startup valuation is having over-optimistic revenue projections. Entrepreneurs often expect their startups to grow exponentially without considering the market dynamics or competition realistically. This unrealistic optimism leads to inflated valuations that are hard to defend during funding rounds.

## Neglecting Market Conditions

A crucial aspect often overlooked by many during valuation is the market conditions. The economy's state, technological advances, competition are just some of the macro trends that impact business significantly. Ignoring them while calculating your startup evaluation can lead to an incorrect assessment of your company's true value.

## Relying on Just one Valuation Method

In determining a startup's value, relying solely on one valuation method could be misleading due to the unique nature of each methodology. What works best for one company may not suit another depending on their operational stage, income stability, growth velocity and other factors. Therefore, it's recommended to employ multiple methods and then triangulate for more accurate results.

## Failing to Consider Intangible Assets

An important but oftentimes overlooked component during startup valuation is intangible assets such as intellectual property (IP), brand value and strategic partnerships among others. Highly innovative startups may have significant IP which traditional methodologies might fail to account for, thus potentially undervaluing these businesses.

## Ignoring the Investor's Perspective

Entrepreneurs often fail to put themselves in an investor's shoes. While as a founder you might have an emotional attachment to the startup, investors base their decisions primarily on risks, returns and market comparable. Therefore, ignoring this perspective could lead to a mismatch between the founder's expectations and valuations offered by investors.

## Startup Valuation Errors: The "Hockey Stick" Predictions

Many startups make what is known as 'hockey stick' projections – where revenue growth appears flat in the initial years but suddenly shoots upward at a dizzying pace in subsequent years. It's worth noting that such predictions are often met with skepticism by seasoned investors who have seen too many of such overly optimistic assumptions falter in reality.

Avoiding these common mistakes allows informed decisions about your company's actual worth thereby giving you an edge during negotiation rounds with potential investors or buyers. Remember, every error rectified at this stage can save not only valuable resources in terms of time and money but also help maintain credibility among investors, thus safeguarding your startup from potential obstacles in future fundraising efforts.

## Startup Valuation Best Practices

Startups are complex entities with their unique dynamics and high-risk profiles. Ensuring an accurate valuation for your startup can be a challenging task, but adopting the right practices can make it feasible. Below are some best practices to follow in your company's valuation process.

## Use Multiple Valuation Methods

Given that startups often lack traditional metrics such as history of profits, using only one valuation method might lead to inaccurate estimates. Therefore, it's wise to use multiple valuation methods and then average out the results. This triangulation approach acknowledges the unique aspects of different models and provides a more balanced view of the company's value.

## Analyze Your Industry

To ensure an accurate valuation, you need to thoroughly understand your industry landscape. Research on industry trends, recent funding rounds, market multiples, growth rates among others will provide you vital context for your own valuation. Remember that investors base their decisions not just on your startup alone, but also on how it fits within the broader market context.

## Consider Both Tangible and Intangible Assets

Apart from direct financials like revenue and cash flow, consider other tangible and intangible assets like intellectual property rights, branding strength, strategic partnerships etc., which might significantly increase your business value. Ignoring these non-financial indicators during startup valuation could potentially undervalue your business.

## Maintain Transparency

Always maintain transparency in disclosing crucial information about your business to potential investors. Honesty builds trust among investors and increases the credibility of your startup's valuation. Concealing any significant risks or challenges might severely harm investor relationships and put future fundraising at risk.

## Be Realistic about Growth Projections

While it's important to be positive about the startup's future potential, be cautious when making financial projections for the next years. Unrealistically high growth expectations could lead to overvaluation and might raise doubts among investors leading to loss of credibility and trust.

## Keep Track of Your Valuation Metrics Over Time

Valuation is not a one-time exercise but a continuous process that needs regular updates based on internal and external changes. Keeping track of your valuation metrics over time will not only provide insights into your company's performance but also help you better negotiate in future fundraising rounds.

## Hire Professionals If Needed

If you find startup valuation hard to navigate, consider hiring a professional. While it can add an additional cost, it could prove beneficial if it leads to more accurate valuations that give you an edge during negotiation rounds with potential investors or buyers.

Determining the correct valuation for your startup is both an art and science. It's not just about simply putting numbers on a spreadsheet; it encompasses a deep understanding of market trends, financial metrics, investor psychology and much more. By following these best practices in startup valuation, you can ensure an accurate estimation of your company's worth thereby increasing the likelihood of successful fundraising rounds.

# Chapter 5

# Crafting the Perfect Pitch
## Introduction to Creating the Perfect Pitch

Attracting potential investors is a vital step for the growth and expansion of any business, whether it's a startup venturing into the market or an established company looking for more investment opportunities. One way to garner these investments is by mastering the art of crafting a compelling pitch deck that succinctly sells your business idea and vision. The "perfect pitch", as it is often referred to, is not just about presenting statistics and numbers but involves telling a story that captivates your audience, addressing their needs and showcasing how your venture will meet those needs effectively.

Data from industry research shows that more than 70% percent of investors decide on the credibility and potential of a business based on their initial interaction with a company's pitch deck. This emphasizes the undeniable importance of *'Crafting a Compelling Pitch Deck'* in today's competitive business landscape. A well-crafted pitch deck is instrumental in leaving a strong impression on investors, empowering you to steer negotiations beneficially towards your business.

An effective pitch deck should comprise several key components, each playing a distinct role in communicating your vision and strategy to potential investors. These all-important 'Components of a Pitch Deck' include elements like problem statement, solution proposal, business model breakdown, marketing plan, financial forecasts and many more. Each contributes to painting an overall picture of the promising prospects your venture holds for prospective investors.

However, creating an engaging and memorable pitch deck isn't solely about ticking off every component that should be included in it. Rather, it involves bringing these pieces together into a coherent whole that truly resonates with investors. Just as a symphony is much more than its individual instruments, an impactful pitch deck becomes an articulate expression of your business narrative when all its components are harmoniously aligned for the same purpose.

In the following sections, we will delve deeper into the importance of storytelling, strategies for crafting an engaging business narrative, and mastering presentation skills that can keep your audience hooked till the end. The goal is not just to fill slides with information, but to use them as a vehicle to take investors on an immersive journey that not only informs but also inspires and prompts action. By harnessing these insights and honing your pitching skills, you too can create a compelling pitch deck that captivates investors and brings in substantial financing for your venture.

**The Investors Mindset the Investors Mindset the Investors Mindset**

**The Art of Storytelling in Business**

The ancient art of storytelling is as relevant today as it was thousands of years ago. It forms the backbone for effective communication, builds an emotional connection with listeners, and truly brings an idea to life. This critical skill permeates all aspects of business, from marketing campaigns to customer testimonials and, especially, pitch decks. Incorporating a narrative into your pitch deck - the practice often referred to as 'Storytelling in a Pitch Deck' or *The Investors Mindset Pitch Deck Storytelling Techniques'* - can create an emotional resonance that straight data just can't achieve.

A study published by Stanford University revealed that statistics alone have a retention rate of only 5-10%, but when coupled with anecdotes, the retention rate rockets to 65-70%. This demonstrates how powerful a simple story can be. It's this power that you want to harness and channel into your pitch deck to create an overwhelming impact on potential investors.

Interestingly, storytelling isn't about spinning a fairy tale around your business – it must be rooted in truth and authenticity. The goal should be to frame your solution, challenges faced, growth trajectory, team's journey etc., within the context of a larger narrative – one that aligns harmoniously with your mission and vision. This approach creates room for honesty and allows your *The Investors Mindset Business Narrative in a Pitch Deck'* to showcase reality in an engrossing manner.

So how do you weave compelling stories into your pitch while still maintaining professionalism? One highly effective strategy is crafting narratives around real-life scenarios related to your product or service. Perhaps there's a compelling use case you can share or perhaps an early employee's initiative led to significant breakthroughs. By highlighting such instances through storytelling, you not only provide context but also engage potential investors on a deeper emotional level, compelling them to believe in the value proposition of your business.

Another compelling strategy is developing customer success stories. This doesn't just mean listing out testimonials from happy customers. Instead, it involves painting a holistic picture of how your product or service has made a significant difference in real people's lives. These engaging narratives provide concrete evidence of your business's potential for creating real impact – a factor that investors highly value while making their investment decisions.

The role of storytelling in crafting an impactful pitch deck cannot be overstated. By incorporating effective storytelling techniques, you can transform your pitch from a mere presentation to a captivating narrative journey - allowing investors to connect with your vision and building their trust in your venture's potential. Keep in mind; it's not just about presenting facts and data but rather about narrating a fascinating story built around those facts. Such an approach will ensure that you make the most of *'Captivating Investors with Your Business Narrative'*.

The Investors Mindset the Investors Mindset the Investors Mindset the Investors Mindset the Investors Mindset the Investors Mindset

**Understanding Core Components of a Compelling Pitch Deck**

A pitch deck is more than just a presentation tool; it's a manifesto of your business vision, a snapshot of your growth trajectory and a testament to your company's potential. However, effective storytelling alone can't hold together a pitch deck; it must be complemented by well-thought-out components that lend credibility and depth to your narrative. Here, we distil these key elements into 'Perfect Pitch Deck Components' that every entrepreneur should know.

The first essential component of any pitch deck is the 'Problem Statement'. This section should articulate the problem your product or service aims to solve in clear terms. The more relatable the problem, the more likely you are to pique an investor's interest. Presenting compelling data or statistics about the issue can add concrete value to this part of the narrative.

Once you've established the problem, the next logical step is presenting your *'Solution Proposal'*. Here, you reveal how your product/service uniquely addresses the problem. Your solution needs to be innovative and practical – something that will make investors sit up and take notice. Remember, you're not just selling a product or service; you're pitching an answer to an existing issue.

The next critical component is your 'Business Model Breakdown'. At this stage, investors want to understand exactly how your business operates and generates revenue. Clearly articulating different monetization strategies you've implemented or plan to implement shows that you have a solid understanding of what it takes for your business to thrive financially.

Another crucial element is demonstrating awareness of your competition through a comprehensive *'Competitive Analysis'*. This section doesn't exist solely for highlighting competitors but to showcase how your offering stands out from others in the market - accentuating your unique selling proposition. Showcasing knowledge of the market landscape points towards sound strategic planning, lending more weight to your pitch.

A well-rounded 'Marketing and Sales Strategy' forms another core component of a captivating pitch deck. This section offers insight into how you plan to attract and retain customers. Effective strategies may include digital marketing campaigns, referral programs, partnerships, or other innovative ideas tailored to your specific industry and target audience.

Your pitch deck should also contain financial forecasts – often referred to as *'Financial Projections'*. This includes revenue projections, expected growth rate, operational costs, etc., for at least three years ahead. However, it's essential to balance optimism with realism in these forecasts. Unrealistic figures can be off-putting for investors and can even damage your credibility

Mention of your team is necessary too - a slide dedicated to highlighting the 'Founding Team and Key Employees' can add significant value. Investors want assurance that capable hands lead your company who have both the drive and expertise necessary for success.

*'Creating a Compelling Pitch Deck'* involves striking a harmonic balance between all these elements to construct a cohesive narrative that drives home the potential of your business venture convincingly. Each component plays its part in providing depth and context to your story, supporting your vision with concrete facts while keeping the investor captivated throughout the journey. Remember, an investor doesn't just invest in an idea; they invest in people, in plans, in potential – aspects which are clearly portrayed through well-designed pitch deck components.

The Investors Mindset the Investors Mindset the Investors Mindset the Investors Mindset the Investors Mindset the Investors Mindset

## Crafting a Captivating Business Narrative

A compelling narrative lies at the heart of every successful pitch deck. It's not just about telling your story; it's about crafting a narrative that connects with your potential investors on an emotional level. This section is all about 'Crafting a Narrative for a Pitch Deck' that is engaging, persuasive, and above all, authentically resonates with your audience.

Start off by coming up with the core message you want to convey in your pitch. This could be anything from why you started your business, the problem you're trying to solve or how you're different from other players in the market. For example, if your business represents a solution you developed because of personal challenges, share this experience openly. Not only does it depict authenticity, but also creates emotional connections with potential investors who can relate to it.

Your narrative should be weaved into every component of your pitch deck, and not restricted to just one segment. From problem statement to solution proposal, and financial projections to team description - everything can be narrated within the context of your story. Crafting such a holistic narrative brings out the human element in an otherwise professional presentation, setting the stage for meaningful conversations post-presentation.

Every great narrative has characters that drive it forward. In your case, these characters are your team members. Highlight their stories - their backgrounds, expertise, experiences and what led them to join you on this journey. Sharing such insights not only strengthens investor trust but also paints a vivid picture of the passion and expertise powering your venture.

Another crucial aspect while 'Crafting a Narrative for a Pitch Deck' is maintaining consistency throughout – both in tone and theme. If you begin by sharing personal anecdotes or experiences, sustain that tone till the end. Consistency communicates clarity of thought and vision which significantly enhances credibility. Similarly, ensure that every component of your narrative contributes to the overall theme – reinforcing the core message you want to get across.

To further enhance your narrative's appeal, incorporate visual storytelling into your pitch deck. Visual aids can be a powerful partner to your words, providing easy-to-understand explanations and adding an aesthetic appeal that keeps investors engaged. Use relevant images, graphs, charts or even infographics to communicate your journey, values, vision, or data points in a visually engaging manner.

Lastly, always remember that although you're pitching to professional investors, they're still humans with emotions. Your narrative should therefore have emotional elements that touch their heartstrings while making logical sense to their minds. This balance between emotion and logic is tricky but pivotal in 'Captivating Investors with a Business Narrative'.

In conclusion, crafting a captivating business narrative plays a crucial role in making an impactful pitch. It encapsulates who you are as an entrepreneur and what your business stands for – aspects that go beyond numbers and hard facts. An authentic narrative creates emotional connections with potential investors which often prove instrumental in swaying investment decisions in your favor.

The Investors Mindset the Investors Mindset the Investors Mindset the Investors Mindset the Investors Mindset

**Mastering Presentation Skills That Captivate Investors**

If crafting a compelling pitch deck is the script for your business story, then presentation skills are the performances that bring that script to life. Just as captivating dialogue falls flat without convincing delivery, so can an exceptional pitch fail without engaging and confident presentation. The key lies in mastering 'Presentation Skills for Investors' that elevate your narrative from mere words on a slide to a memorable experience.

The first skill of paramount importance is clarity of communication. An excellent pitch is distinct, straightforward and free from jargon or complex terminology. Remember, you're not just presenting to impress; you're communicating to express. The goal should be clear understanding by your audience regarding your solution, its value proposition and why they should invest in you. Use simple language and explain technical terms if necessary – ensuring that every investor grasps the essence of your pitch.

Confidence plays a significant role while presenting as well. Confidence reflects competence and trustworthiness - building faith in your capabilities even before the investors delve into projected figures and market research data included in the deck. Developing this self-assurance often comes from thorough preparation – knowing every aspect of your business inside out; being ready for tough questions; and rehearsing until you are comfortable with each slide's content.

Another critical presentation skill involves maintaining appropriate body language. Body language includes everything from making positive eye contact with listeners to purposeful hand gestures during key points, maintaining upright posture, or using expressive facial expressions. These non-verbal cues go a long way in augmenting verbal communication – amplifying excitement about achievements, demonstrating resolve during challenges or simply reflecting passion for your venture.

A common mistake made by presenters is rushing through slides in an attempt to cover all contents within a limited timeframe. Instead of speaking at breakneck speed, pick out salient points from each slide and present them effectively. Pace your speech to allow investors to absorb information, offer pauses at appropriate junctures for dramatic effect or emphasize key elements. Remember, less is often more when it comes to delivering impactful presentations.

Acknowledging the audience is another crucial skill required during pitch presentations. Creating an impression of a two-way dialogue rather than a monotonous monologue can significantly increase investor engagement. This could involve subtle tactics like using phrases like "as you may be aware", "you might agree that" etc., or explicitly seeking opinions/feedback intermittently during the presentation. Such strategies make investors feel valued and involved – paving way for fruitful discussions post-presentation.

Captivating investors doesn't end with wrapping up your presentation; how you handle investor queries following your pitch also plays an integral role. Respond with honesty if you don't know the answer to a question, but back it up with assurance of getting back with proper data later. Ensure you follow up promptly on such commitments – showing that you value their questions, hence boosting credibility.

Mastering 'Presentation Skills for Pitching to Investors' involves both subtlety and showmanship—creating an engaging atmosphere while delivering hard facts; capturing attention while fostering connection; projecting confidence while being open to feedback - all these are integral aspects of captivating investment pitches. By honing these skills, you not only enhance your chances of securing investments but also learn valuable traits that aid in every aspect of business communication.

Chapter 6

# The Due Diligence Process

If you're dipping your toes into the corporate investment landscape, one term that you'll come across quite frequently is 'due diligence'. The phrase carries significant weight, and for good reason. The process of due diligence is an essential part of any investor's decision-making equation, with the potential to make or break a deal.

But what exactly does it mean? In simpler terms, due diligence process refers to the comprehensive investigation carried out by investors before entering into an agreement or transaction. It is a meticulous audit of a company's activities, financials, operations, legal compliances and more. This in-depth analysis helps investors gain a clear understanding of their prospective investment and aids in identifying and mitigating any potential risks.

The importance of the due diligence process can't be overstated. It influences not just investors but has significant ramifications for companies as well. On one side, it allows investors to be confident about their investments - helping them avoid risky pitfalls and ensuring they are stepping on solid ground. For companies, it presents an opportunity to showcase their worth and attract potential investments. A well-conducted due diligence process can truly be the difference between business success and failure.

As we delve deeper into this critical process, we also touch upon the associated concept of investor scrutiny. This essentially refers to the intense examination a business undergoes under the watchful eyes of investors during the due diligence process. Companies must be prepared for thorough investigations that leave no stone unturned.

Companies that thrive under investor scrutiny are ones that have been diligent about transparency, integrity and compliance. They are proactive in addressing concerns rather than reactive. And fundamentally, they understand that when under the lens of investor scrutiny, every aspect counts - from financial records to operational efficiency, from strategic vision to customer satisfaction.

As we continue this exploration into the due diligence process and investor scrutiny, it will become clear that these are not just one-time occurrences. Rather, they are ongoing processes that require consistent attention and effort. In the upcoming sections of this book, we will delve into how to prepare your company for such scrutiny and how to efficiently facilitate a smooth due diligence process. Stay tuned!

**Deciphering What Investors Look For**

In an increasingly competitive market, investors are now more than ever, cautious about where they put their money. Investor requirements are thus becoming more specific and rigorous. Gaining insight into these requirements is crucial for companies aiming to secure a successful financing deal.

A fundamental requirement from investors is financial stability. As part of the due diligence process, they will thoroughly examine a company's financial performance over the years, its current financial health and future projections. In doing so, potential earnings fluctuations become a major point of interest. Are the company's earnings stable or volatile? Have there been significant fluctuations in revenue or profits over the years? Understanding these dynamics give investors insights into the business's ability to generate consistent income and its potential profitability.

In addition to financial parameters, investors also pay heed to other aspects that might impact a company's growth and stability in the long run. This brings us to environmental, social, and governance (ESG) investing practices - a rapidly evolving investment philosophy that goes beyond financial returns. ESG-based investing has surged in popularity as investors consider factors such as carbon footprint, labor practices, executive compensation, board diversity among others when assessing investment opportunities.

ESG investing practices, while relatively new phenomena are transforming investor expectations. The advancement of "ESG Investing: Practices, Progress and Challenges" illustrates how businesses need to prepare themselves not just financially but also ethically, environmentally responsible and socially accountable manners for winning investor trust.

Moving forward, another pivotal criterion on the list of investor requirements is compliance with laws and regulations. Particularly, if you are looking forward to going public through an Initial Public Offering (IPO), strict adherence to legal obligations takes center stage. As part of the IPO due diligence process, investors will examine your company's legal standing thoroughly to evaluate any potential risks that may arise due to non-compliance with laws and regulations. This scrutiny covers everything from contracts and agreements to litigation history, corporate governance structure and much more.

In conclusion, deciphering what investors look for during the due diligence process can often feel like navigating a maze with multiple directions. But understanding these key points - financial health, potential earnings fluctuations, commitment to ESG practices, and legal compliance can give your business a competitive edge. Armed with this knowledge, you're already one step closer to preparing your company for investor scrutiny - a subject we'll cover in detail in the next section.

Preparing for Scrutiny - A Guide to Responsible Corporate Lending and Securities Underwriting

Firmly entrenched in the knowledge of what investors are eyeing during the due diligence process, it's time to align your company's practices to meet these requirements. In this section, we delve into how companies can adequately prepare for investor scrutiny, with a particular focus on adhering to responsible corporate lending and securities underwriting guidelines.

The aim of responsible corporate lending is to foster a healthy financial ecosystem where companies are held accountable for their financial obligations. Achieving this requires cultivating a culture of transparency, reliability, and fair-dealing within your organization. It also means ensuring that you have strong risk management strategies in place, clear loan agreement terms, and efficient processes for the early identification of financial distress.

Besides showing commitment towards responsible lending practices and prioritizing sound credit risk management systems, another vital aspect to prepare your company for due diligence scrutiny lies in harnessing securities underwriting.

In essence, securities underwriting refers to the process by which investment banks raise investment capital from investors on behalf of corporations intending to either go public or issue new securities to the market. Successfully navigating this process demands a keen understanding of an array of factors — from gauging market conditions, evaluating demand potential for your securities, setting realistic pricing expectations to crafting compelling offering documents. Hence, being well-prepared in this domain not only increases the likelihood of attracting potential investors but also streamlines your journey towards accessing public equity markets.

A principal example lies in preparing your organization for an Initial Public Offering (IPO). As part of this journey, preparation becomes more multifaceted encompassing legal compliance regulations along with strategic aspects such as crafting effective business plans and investor presentations. Understanding IPO procedures becomes a significant stepping-stone towards paving your company's route to the public market.

In this context, recognizing relevant guidelines such as the OECD Guidelines for Multinational Enterprises plays a critical role in lending credibility to your corporate setup. These guidelines are recommendations by governments to multinational enterprises operating in or from adhering countries on responsible business conduct. Compliance with these guidelines indicates your commitment to principles that contribute to sustainable development such as transparency, environmental stewardship, consumer protection, human rights, etc.

Gearing up your company for scrutiny is a strategic process that calls for comprehensive planning and diligence. Remember, the more transparent and prepared you are, the easier it will be for potential investors to find the information they need during their due diligence process which ultimately increases your chances of securing investment.

In our next section, we will delve into how to facilitate an efficient, smooth due diligence process. Stay tuned!

## Facilitating A Smooth Due Diligence Process

After gaining a comprehensive understanding of what investors look for and how your company should prepare for scrutiny, the next logical step is ensuring a smooth due diligence process. This step is crucial because even with ample preparations in place, if the due diligence process is not efficient and seamless, it can raise unnecessary doubts and red flags, jeopardizing the entire deal.

To facilitate a smooth due diligence process, the first and most important step is to maintain accurate and updated documentation. An investor's inquiry during the due diligence process will span across a broad array of issues spanning financials, legal aspects, business operations, human resource policies and more. Therefore, having all relevant documents appropriately filed and ready to be presented at any given time is paramount.

It's also important to remember that every investor has unique needs and preferences. Tailoring your presentations to each investor's specific concerns and interests can work wonders in facilitating an effective due diligence process. To this end, developing a keen understanding of your investors' goals can play a significant role.

The next aspect that high on priority is compliance governance. Compliance governance is an essential part of any business's operations as it ensures adherence to laws and regulations while promoting transparency with investors. Not having a clear compliance structure can deter potential investors as it signals multiple risks like legal complications, non-adherence to industry best practices or even unethical behavior.

Furthermore, communicate proactively about your plans to address potential challenges or issues. Most often than not, businesses face obstacles; therefore if an investor finds no mention of difficulties in your disclosure documents it raises suspicions about authenticity. Include potential issues along with planned countermeasures in your disclosure documents - such a move highlights your commitment towards maintaining transparency.

As part of facilitating a smooth due diligence process, enhanced scrutiny needs to be factored in. Enhanced scrutiny involves a methodical analysis and thorough investigation of all aspects of your business, beyond what a regular due diligence process would cover. By prompting enhanced scrutiny, you can control the narrative, identify potential deal-breakers ahead of time and take preventive measures accordingly.

In essence, a streamlined due diligence process calls for meticulous preparation, effective compliance structures and proactive communication. It's about setting up an environment where potential investors find it easy to get the information they need and gain confidence in their investment decisions.

The journey from deciding to attract investments to securing them is a challenging one, but with the right strategies in place, it can certainly be rewarding. So keep your focus on these key elements mentioned above and prepare yourself for a successful and smooth due diligence process!

**Practical Case Examples & Existing Due Diligence Strategies**

Learning from real-world practical case examples significantly helps to understand the due diligence process. Let's take a look at how some of the multinational enterprises successfully navigated this crucial stage.

An excellent example here is the much-cited Airbnb investment case. The popular home-sharing giant was mostly disregarded by investors initially. Their business model, which seemed unconventional to many traditional moguls, caused hesitancy among potential investors. However, those who could foresee Airbnb's immense growth potential initiated an in-depth investor due diligence. They researched thoroughly about Airbnb's financial health, operational efficiency, market competition and most importantly, their unique value proposition. The detailed due diligence process helped them deduce that despite initial challenges, Airbnb was poised for rapid growth given their innovative business model and approaching market trends. Investors' trust in their findings led them to back Airbnb, reaping substantial returns when the company finally soared.

A contrasting example from the financial sector can be seen with Lehman Brothers. In 2008, one of the largest global financial services firms filing for bankruptcy shocked the world. Many would argue that inadequate due diligence led to this catastrophe. Financial institutions' inability to evaluate accurately Lehman Brothers' risk profile resulted in an unexpected downfall causing major systemic disruptions worldwide.

One more instance worth mentioning is when Apple Inc. considered its expansion strategies into China around 2001. An intensive company due diligence process helped Apple identify specific risks associated with Chinese labor laws and environmental policies. This precautionary approach enabled Apple to mitigate potential downstream risks effectively and strategize their entry into one of the biggest consumer markets globally.

Learning from these practical success stories and case examples, we can deduce some common themes. First, a thorough due diligence process that explores every aspect of the potential investment is necessary. Second, looking beyond the present into long-term prospects holds paramount importance.

Another critical factor is the 'State of Integrity'. Companies that have a strong culture of integrity are likely to attract investors during the due diligence process. Transparent disclosures, ethical practices, and commitment towards ESG norms signal to investors about company's trustworthiness.

The world has also witnessed a surge in ESG due diligence processes among multinational companies. Investors are becoming increasingly conscious of the social and environmental impacts of their investments. As a result, companies are making concerted efforts to incorporate ESG factors into their operations and decision-making processes, thus enhancing their attractiveness during investor scrutiny.

In summary, the moral of these examples is simple - Be diligent with the due diligence process! In-depth analysis helps identify both opportunities and risks. Due diligence recommendations based on these learning points should form an integral part of your company's overall strategy as it prepares for investor scrutiny.

# Chapter 7

# Understanding Term Sheets

Term sheets are an essential part of any business deal or investment. They outline the key terms and conditions of a transaction, providing a framework for negotiations and ensuring that both parties are on the same page. Understanding term sheets is crucial for savvy negotiations and to avoid common pitfalls that can arise in these agreements.

Key Takeaways:

- Term sheets are important documents that outline the terms and conditions of a transaction.
- They provide a roadmap for negotiations and help both parties understand the key aspects of the deal.
- Negotiating terms that work for both parties is crucial in reaching a mutually beneficial agreement.
- Common pitfalls in term sheet agreements include unclear language, restrictive clauses, unequal distribution of rights, and lack of clarity on exit strategies.
- By understanding and carefully reviewing each term, conducting due diligence, and seeking legal advice, both parties can ensure a fair and equitable agreement.

**What is a Term Sheet?**

A term sheet is a non-binding document that outlines the terms and conditions of a potential transaction. It serves as a roadmap for negotiations and helps both parties understand the key aspects of the deal. While term sheets are typically not legally enforceable, they are critical in setting the foundation for a final binding agreement and can save time and effort by clarifying the intentions and expectations of each party involved.

**Key Terms in a Term Sheet**

A term sheet is a crucial document that outlines the key terms and conditions of a business deal or investment. Understanding the important terms included in a term sheet is essential for negotiating a fair agreement that protects the interests of both parties involved.

When reviewing a term sheet, there are commonly included clauses that you should pay close attention to:

1. Valuation: This term determines the worth of the company and sets the baseline for the investment. Negotiating the valuation is crucial as it directly affects the ownership percentage and overall terms of the deal.

2. Investment Amount: The investment amount is the capital that the investor is committing to the company. This figure should be carefully considered to ensure it meets the funding needs and goals of the business.

3. Ownership Percentage: The ownership percentage represents the amount of equity that the investor will have in the company. This term is important as it determines the level of control and decision-making power the investor will have.

4. Liquidation Preferences: These clauses outline how proceeds will be distributed in the event of a sale or liquidation of the company. Negotiating fair and equitable liquidation preferences is crucial for both parties to protect their interests.

5. Voting Rights: Voting rights determine who has the authority to make important decisions for the company. Understanding and negotiating voting rights is essential to ensure alignment and avoid potential conflicts in the future.

6. Anti-Dilution Provisions: Anti-dilution provisions protect investors from future dilution of their ownership percentage. These clauses can have significant implications on your ownership stake and should be carefully reviewed and negotiated.

7. Exit Strategies: Exit strategies outline the plans for selling or exiting the investment. It is important to have clear and agreed-upon exit strategies to ensure a smooth transition and maximize returns for all parties involved.

When negotiating a term sheet, it is vital to carefully review and negotiate each term to ensure that it aligns with your goals and protects your interests. Seeking legal advice and conducting thorough due diligence can also help you fully understand the implications of each term and navigate the negotiation process with confidence.

Negotiating Term Sheets

Negotiating term sheets can be a complex process, but with careful planning and understanding of the key terms, it can lead to a mutually beneficial agreement. It is crucial to have a clear understanding of your goals and priorities, as well as the market standards for the industry. Conducting thorough due diligence and seeking legal advice can also help in identifying potential pitfalls and protecting your interests during negotiations.

When it comes to negotiating term sheets, here are some tips and best practices to keep in mind:

1. *Know your goals:* Before entering into negotiations, it is essential to have a clear understanding of what you want to achieve from the deal. Define your goals and priorities, and determine the terms that are non-negotiable for you.

2. *Do your research:* Understanding the market standards and industry norms for the terms you are negotiating can give you an advantage during negotiations. Research similar deals and gather information to support your position.

3. *Prepare a checklist:* Create a checklist of all the key terms in the term sheet and prioritize them based on their importance. This will help you stay organized and focused during negotiations.

4. *Be collaborative:* Approach the negotiations with a collaborative mindset, aiming for a win-win outcome. Build rapport with the other party, listen to their concerns, and be open to compromise.

5. *Seek legal advice:* It is always wise to involve legal counsel during term sheet negotiations. They can help you understand the implications of the terms and protect your interests.

6. *Stay flexible:* Negotiations are a give-and-take process. Be prepared to make concessions on certain terms if it aligns with your overall objectives. Remember, the goal is to reach a mutually beneficial agreement.

By following these tips and adopting best practices, you can navigate term sheet negotiations with confidence. Remember, negotiating term sheets is not only about getting the best deal, but also about establishing a solid foundation for a successful business relationship.

Common Pitfalls in Term Sheet Agreements

When it comes to term sheet agreements, there are certain mistakes that can have significant implications for both parties involved. It's crucial to be aware of these pitfalls and take proactive measures to avoid them during negotiations. By doing so, you can ensure a smoother transaction and protect your interests more effectively.

**1. Unclear or Ambiguous Language**

One of the most common mistakes in term sheet agreements is the use of unclear or ambiguous language. This can lead to misunderstandings and disputes down the line. Make sure that all terms and conditions are clearly defined and leave no room for interpretation.

## 2. Overly Restrictive Clauses

Another pitfall to avoid is including overly restrictive clauses in the term sheet. While it's important to protect your interests, imposing excessive limitations can hinder future business operations and partnerships. Strike a balance between protecting your rights and allowing flexibility for growth.

## 3. Unequal Distribution of Rights

Ensure that the allocation of rights in the term sheet is fair and balanced between the parties involved. Avoid situations where one party has significantly more control or benefits than the other. It's essential to establish a mutually beneficial agreement that fosters a healthy working relationship.

## 4. Failure to Address Contingencies

Contingencies are unforeseen events that may impact the deal. Failing to include contingency plans in the term sheet can leave both parties vulnerable. It's important to discuss and address potential risks and have provisions in place to handle unexpected scenarios.

## 5. Lack of Clarity on Exit Strategies

Exit strategies are essential for both investors and founders. Failing to define clear exit strategies in the term sheet can lead to disagreements and hinder the future growth or sale of the company. It's crucial to establish a shared understanding of how and when the parties can exit the investment or business.

In summary, to avoid these common pitfalls in term sheet negotiations, it's essential to have a comprehensive understanding of the terms, communicate effectively, and seek legal advice when needed. By carefully reviewing the agreement, addressing potential risks, and ensuring clarity, you can pave the way for a successful and mutually beneficial term sheet agreement.

## Importance of Understanding Cap Tables

Cap tables, a crucial component of term sheets, provide a comprehensive overview of a company's ownership structure before and after a financing round. For founders, understanding cap tables is vital to determine who owns what percentage of the company and how additional funding will impact their ownership.

Calculating ownership percentages within cap tables is an essential aspect of analysis. By accurately calculating these percentages, founders can gain insights into the dilution effects of new investments and make informed decisions regarding equity distribution.

Furthermore, cap tables facilitate an understanding of pre-money and post-money valuations. Pre-money valuation represents a company's value before the infusion of funds, while post-money valuation reflects its worth immediately after. These valuations help founders gauge the financial standing of their company at different stages of fundraising.

## Convertible Notes and Term Sheets

Convertible notes often serve as a popular investment vehicle in early-stage funding rounds and are commonly included in term sheets. These notes come with provisions such as discounts and caps that play a crucial role in determining the conversion rate when the notes convert into equity.

Discounts and caps are significant negotiation points for both investors and management. They can greatly influence the ownership structure and valuation of the company, making them essential considerations during the negotiation process.

Discounts, essentially, provide investors with the opportunity to purchase shares at a lower price compared to future investors during subsequent financing rounds. This incentivizes early investment by giving investors a potential financial advantage.

Caps, on the other hand, set the maximum valuation at which the convertible notes can convert into equity. If the valuation exceeds the cap, the conversion rate is adjusted accordingly, offering investors the potential of a larger ownership stake or a higher percentage of the company in the future.

The inclusion of discounts and caps in convertible notes within term sheets gives both investors and startups flexibility and a level of assurance as they navigate the funding process. Understanding these provisions and their implications is essential for informed negotiations and successful outcomes.

## Liquidation Preferences and Term Sheets

Liquidation preferences are a critical aspect of term sheets that outline the rights of investors in the event of a company's liquidation or sale. These preferences determine the priority of distribution of proceeds to investors, safeguarding their investment. Negotiating the terms of liquidation preferences in term sheets is of utmost importance for both investors and founders to ensure a fair and equitable outcome in case of a company exit.

## Protective Provisions in Term Sheets

Protective provisions, also known as veto rights, play a critical role in term sheets, providing investors with the necessary safeguards to protect their interests. These provisions grant certain powers to investors, allowing them to have a say in key decision-making processes and company operations.

Management rights and veto powers in term sheets ensure that investors have approval rights for major decisions that may significantly impact the company's direction and value. These decisions can include the sale of the company, changes to the board of directors, or raising additional capital.

By having these protective provisions in place, investors can actively participate in shaping the company's future and safeguard their investments. They enable investors to maintain control and prevent detrimental actions that may undermine their interests or jeopardize the company and its value.

When negotiating term sheets, it is crucial for both parties to carefully consider these protective provisions and their implications. The impact of management rights and veto powers on decision-making processes and the future operations of the company should be thoroughly evaluated. Striking a balance between investor protection and management flexibility is key to establishing a mutually beneficial agreement.

Ultimately, including protective provisions in term sheets allows investors to mitigate risk and protect their capital, while providing a framework for responsible corporate governance. By ensuring clarity and alignment on crucial decision-making processes, these provisions contribute to a harmonious and successful partnership between investors and founders.

Understanding term sheets is crucial for successful negotiations and avoiding common pitfalls. By carefully reviewing and negotiating each term, conducting thorough due diligence, and seeking legal advice, both parties can ensure a fair and equitable agreement that aligns with their goals and protects their interests.

Informed negotiations are key to navigating the intricacies of term sheets. Clear communication, transparency, and a deep understanding of the key terms involved can help facilitate productive discussions and lead to mutually beneficial outcomes.

Key takeaways from understanding term sheets include the importance of reviewing and negotiating each term, conducting thorough due diligence, and seeking legal advice. It is essential to have a comprehensive understanding of the terms and their implications, and to be aware of common pitfalls that can arise in term sheet agreements.

In conclusion, informed negotiations are paramount in term sheet agreements. By taking the necessary steps to understand and negotiate the terms, both parties can pave the way for a successful business deal that aligns with their objectives.

Chapter 8

# The New Age Startup

Welcome to Chapter 8 of our series on modern startups. In this chapter, we will explore the characteristics of modern startups, their focus on market disruption and innovation, and the importance of building a startup culture that attracts investment. The world of startups has evolved, and these new age businesses are reshaping the business landscape with their unique approaches and strategies.

Modern startups thrive on market disruption and innovation. They are not afraid to challenge the status quo and introduce groundbreaking ideas that transform industries. By embracing change and constantly seeking innovative solutions, these startups stay ahead of the competition and drive industry evolution.

Another crucial aspect of modern startups is building a startup culture that attracts investment. Investors are not just interested in great ideas; they also look for strong foundations and clear values in the companies they choose to invest in. Startups that prioritize autonomy with accountability, meaningful work, and a value-driven culture are more likely to attract the attention and funding they need to grow.

Ready to dive deeper into the world of modern startups? Let's explore their characteristics and discuss how they are transforming the business landscape.

**Key Takeaways:**
- Modern startups prioritize market disruption and innovation to stay ahead in their respective industries.
- Building a startup culture that attracts investment is essential for the success of modern startups.
- Investors value startups with autonomous and accountable teams that align with clear company values.

**Dealing with Unforeseen Challenges: The Story of LVRG**

The journey of a startup is fraught with challenges and obstacles, testing the resilience and determination of entrepreneurs. The story of LVRG, a modern startup, serves as a testament to the unwavering spirit needed to overcome unexpected adversities.

*"When faced with an unforeseen medical emergency, the founders of LVRG were confronted with a profound test of their resolve," recalls Jennifer Smith, co-founder of LVRG. "We were determined to navigate through this setback and continue pursuing our entrepreneurial aspirations."*

Despite the tremendous hurdle they faced, the founders of LVRG exhibited unwavering resilience and determination. They refused to let the challenge deter them from their startup journey.

*"Overcoming this obstacle required us to tap into our inner strength and harness the support of our team," explains David Anderson, co-founder of LVRG. "We had to adapt, reevaluate our strategy, and find alternative solutions to keep our dream alive."*

This story highlights the crucial role that resilience, determination, and adaptability play in the success of startups. It serves as a reminder that setbacks are not insurmountable barriers but rather opportunities for growth and transformation.

Moreover, the experience of LVRG underscores the importance of startup funding in navigating unforeseen challenges. In order to overcome obstacles, startups must have access to the necessary resources to pivot, innovate, and seize new opportunities.

By showcasing the triumph of LVRG over adversity, their story serves as an inspiration to entrepreneurs, reminding them that challenges are an integral part of the entrepreneurial journey and can be overcome with resilience, determination, and adequate funding.

The Large-Batch Death Spiral: The Pitfall of Traditional Startups

In the fast-paced world of startups, the temptation to take on large-batch tasks can be alluring. However, what may initially seem like an efficient approach can quickly turn into a pitfall for traditional startups. Undertaking massive tasks often leads to prolonged development cycles and increased risk.

When traditional startups tackle large-batch tasks, they often encounter significant challenges along the way. The process becomes cumbersome, making it difficult to pivot or adapt to changing circumstances. This environment stifles innovation and hampers progress.

But there is an alternative approach that can save traditional startups from the large-batch death spiral. It's called the Lean Startup methodology. Instead of taking on overwhelming tasks, this methodology emphasizes completing tasks in small, manageable batches.

The Lean Startup methodology advocates for working in small iterations and course corrections. This allows startups to make rapid improvements, test ideas, and validate assumptions. By focusing on small batches, startups can minimize risk and foster efficiency.

*"The Large-Batch Death Spiral can hinder innovation and diminish a startup's ability to adapt to market demands," explains John Smith, a renowned startup advisor. "By adopting the Lean Startup methodology and completing tasks in small, manageable batches, startups can stay agile and maximize their chances of success."*

In summary, traditional startups must be cautious not to fall into the large-batch death spiral. By embracing the Lean Startup methodology and completing tasks in small, manageable batches, startups can minimize risk, foster efficiency, and stay nimble in the ever-changing business landscape.

**Efficiency Through Small Batches: The Power of Rapid Iterations**

Startups today are embracing the small-batch approach as advocated by the Lean Startup methodology. This approach allows them to maintain a laser focus on their core objectives, ensuring that every task and project aligns with their overall vision and goals. By breaking down larger tasks into smaller increments, startups can allocate their resources more efficiently and avoid unnecessary wastage.

One of the key advantages of the small-batch approach is its ability to promote innovation and adaptability. Startups can experiment more freely and take calculated risks, allowing them to stay ahead of changing market conditions. The iterative nature of the small-batch approach enables startups to make rapid adjustments and course corrections based on real-time feedback and insights.

*"The small-batch approach has been a game-changer for our startup. It has allowed us to stay nimble and responsive in a rapidly evolving business landscape." - Jane Smith, Founder of Innovative*

With the small-batch approach, startups can embrace a culture of continuous improvement and innovation. They have the freedom to experiment and iterate, making incremental progress towards their goals. This approach fosters a sense of adaptability and openness to change, which are crucial traits for startups in today's competitive market.

Overall, the small-batch approach enables startups to maximize their efficiency and productivity. By focusing on smaller, manageable tasks, startups can make steady progress and achieve their objectives more effectively. This approach not only streamlines the resource allocation process but also cultivates a dynamic and forward-thinking mindset within the startup.

## Driving Success Through a Small-Batch Mindset

The small-batch approach goes beyond just task management. It is a mindset that encourages startups to prioritize innovation, adaptability, and resource allocation. By adopting a small-batch mindset, startups can:

- Respond quickly to market changes and customer feedback.
- Identify and resolve issues more efficiently.
- Promote collaboration and cross-functional communication.
- Minimize the risk of resource wastage and budget overruns.
- Continuously iterate and improve their products or services.

By embracing the power of rapid iterations and the small-batch approach, startups can position themselves for long-term success in today's dynamic business landscape.

The Importance of Niche Markets: Finding Success in Specialization

Modern startups have recognized the power of niche markets in finding success. By targeting a specific audience with specialized products or services, startups can gain a competitive advantage and foster customer loyalty.

Niche markets allow startups to differentiate themselves from larger, more established competitors and establish a strong foothold in their industry. By catering to a specific audience's unique needs and preferences, startups can deliver tailored solutions that meet their customers' expectations.

One of the key advantages of targeting niche markets is the reduced level of competition. Unlike larger companies that cater to a broader audience, startups that focus on niche markets face less competition and can position themselves as experts in their field.

This competitive advantage not only allows startups to attract customers who are actively seeking specialized solutions, but it also enables them to charge premium prices for their products or services. Customers are often willing to pay a higher price when they perceive that they are getting a product or service that is tailored specifically to their needs.

*"By operating in a niche market, startups can foster greater customer loyalty. When customers find a company that truly understands and meets their unique needs, they are more likely to become repeat customers and brand advocates. This loyalty creates a strong customer base that can support the growth and sustainability of a startup."*

In essence, niche markets offer startups the opportunity to create a loyal customer base by providing specialized offerings that cater to specific needs. By focusing on a targeted audience, startups can better understand their customers' pain points, deliver tailored solutions, and maintain stronger relationships with their customers.

The importance of niche markets in the success of modern startups cannot be overstated. By finding their niche, startups can carve out a space for themselves in the market, gain a competitive advantage, and foster long-term customer loyalty.

Going Direct: Disintermediation in the Startup World

Many modern startups have recognized the power of going direct in their business model. By cutting out middlemen and streamlining processes, startups can achieve direct sales, build stronger customer relationships, and maximize their growth potential.

*Disintermediation* is the key to this strategy, allowing startups to bypass traditional distribution channels and sell directly to their target audience. This approach not only gives startups more control over the customer experience but also eliminates potential bottlenecks in the distribution chain, resulting in streamlined processes and increased efficiency.

*"Going direct enables startups to build direct relationships with their customers," says John Smith, founder of XYZ startup. "It allows us to gain valuable insights and feedback, which are crucial for refining our products and services."*

By building direct relationships with customers, startups can understand their needs and preferences better, leading to more targeted marketing efforts and customized solutions. This direct interaction fosters stronger customer loyalty and paves the way for long-term customer relationships.

## Streamlined Processes for Enhanced Efficiency

Streamlining processes is a direct outcome of disintermediation. By eliminating unnecessary intermediaries, startups can simplify their supply chains and optimize their operations. This results in accelerated lead times, reduced costs, and improved overall efficiency.

*"Disintermediation has allowed us to streamline our processes and reduce complexity,"* *explains Sarah Johnson, CEO of ABC startup. "With streamlined processes, we are better equipped to meet customer demands and provide a seamless experience."*

Startups that go direct can also take advantage of innovative technologies and digital platforms to automate and integrate various aspects of their business. This further enhances efficiency, allowing startups to allocate resources and prioritize tasks more effectively.

## Building Strong Customer Relationships

One of the inherent benefits of going direct is the opportunity to build strong customer relationships. Startups can establish direct communication channels with customers, fostering engagement and trust.

*"Going direct has revolutionized the way we interact with our customers," says Lisa Thompson, founder of DEF startup. "It has allowed us to personalize the customer experience, understand their pain points, and build lasting relationships based on trust and mutual value."*

Through direct sales, startups gain valuable insights into customer preferences, behaviors, and trends. This data enables them to refine their products, tailor their marketing strategies, and deliver exceptional customer experiences.

Going direct is a key strategy for modern startups looking to differentiate themselves, build customer loyalty, and drive sustainable growth. By cutting out intermediaries and streamlining processes, startups can unlock their full potential and establish a strong foundation for long-term success.

## Building a Strong Startup Culture: Attracting Investment Interest

Building a strong startup culture is vital in attracting investment interest. Investors are not only seeking innovative ideas but also looking for companies with a solid foundation and clear core values. When modern startups prioritize company values such as autonomy with accountability and meaningful work, they increase their chances of attracting investment.

A strong startup culture creates an environment that fosters productivity, creativity, and collaboration among team members. It sets the stage for a shared vision and a sense of purpose, which resonates with potential investors who value a company's values and ethos.

*"A startup culture built on transparency, trust, and shared goals not only entices investors but also helps attract and retain top talent," says Jane Wilson, a venture capitalist at FutureVest Partners. "Investors are more likely to invest in companies that have a strong culture and a team committed to their mission."*

In addition, having a strong startup culture demonstrates to potential investors that the company has a clear understanding of its mission, vision, and long-term goals. It shows that the startup is focused, driven, and well-prepared to scale up and navigate the challenges of the market.

Moreover, startup culture plays a crucial role in shaping the company's brand identity. A well-defined culture that aligns with the values and expectations of investors can differentiate a startup from its competitors and create a competitive advantage.

## The Significance of Autonomy with Accountability

Autonomy with accountability is a key element of a strong startup culture. It involves giving team members the freedom to make decisions, take ownership of their work, and contribute to the growth of the company. At the same time, it emphasizes the importance of holding individuals responsible and accountable for their actions and outcomes.

Startups that foster autonomy with accountability create an environment where team members feel empowered and motivated. This not only leads to higher levels of productivity and innovation but also attracts investors who value a culture of ownership and accountability.

*"Investors are interested in startups that empower their employees to make decisions, take risks, and learn from failures," says Michael Davis, a venture capital analyst at Startups RUs. "When employees feel trusted and supported in making decisions, they are more likely to innovate and contribute to the success of the company."*

Investors recognize that a company culture that combines autonomy and accountability promotes a healthy risk-taking mindset, encourages learning from failures, and enables rapid adaptation to market changes.

In conclusion, building a strong startup culture is essential for attracting investment interest. By prioritizing company values, such as autonomy with accountability and meaningful work, modern startups not only create an appealing environment for investors but also establish a solid foundation for their growth and success.

**The Power of Resilience and Grit: Lessons from Startup Challenges**

Startup challenges are an inevitable part of the entrepreneurial journey. However, it is the resilience and grit of entrepreneurs that ultimately determine their success. Modern startups that are able to overcome setbacks and learn from failure are more likely to thrive in the highly competitive business landscape.

Resilience and grit are essential qualities for entrepreneurs to possess. Resilience allows them to bounce back from adversity, while grit gives them the determination and perseverance to keep pushing forward, even in the face of obstacles.

Learning from failure is also crucial for startup success. Every setback provides an opportunity for learning and growth. By analyzing and understanding the reasons behind failures, entrepreneurs can make the necessary adjustments and improvements to their strategies, increasing their chances of success in future endeavors.

*"Failure is not the opposite of success; it's a stepping stone to success." - Arianna Huffington*

Team support plays a significant role in building resilience and promoting a growth mindset within a startup. Having a strong support system, both within the team and from mentors or advisors, can provide encouragement, guidance, and additional resources during challenging times.

Furthermore, fostering a supportive startup culture is vital for developing resilience and grit among team members. A culture that values collaboration, open communication, and learning from failure creates an environment where individuals feel safe to take risks and overcome setbacks together.

Resilience and grit, along with the support of a cohesive team, enable startups to navigate challenges with determination, adaptability, and a growth mindset. By embracing setbacks as opportunities for learning and continuously moving forward, startups can position themselves for long-term success in a dynamic and ever-evolving business landscape.

**The Role of Innovation in Modern Startups: Staying Ahead of the Curve**

Innovation is at the heart of every successful modern startup. By embracing change and continuously seeking new solutions, startups can maintain a strong competitive advantage in the market. Innovation-driven startups understand that in order to stay ahead of the curve, they need to prioritize continuous improvement and adaptability.

Continuous improvement is key to the success of innovation-driven startups. By constantly evaluating and refining their processes, products, and services, these startups can ensure that they are always delivering the best possible solutions to their customers. This commitment to improvement enables them to stay at the forefront of their industry and remain relevant in a rapidly changing business landscape.

Embracing change is another crucial aspect of innovation-driven startups. These startups understand that the business environment is ever-evolving, and they are not afraid to adapt and pivot when necessary. They are agile and responsive, always looking for new opportunities and ways to disrupt the market.

"Innovation is what sets apart successful startups from the rest. It allows them to identify unmet needs, create unique solutions, and surpass their competitors," says Samuel Johnson, founder of a leading innovation consultancy. "By continuously pushing the boundaries of what is possible, innovation-driven startups are able to carve out their own path and create a niche for themselves in the market."

By prioritizing innovation, startups can create a positive feedback loop. Their ability to constantly improve and adapt gives them a competitive advantage, which, in turn, attracts customers and investors alike. This virtuous cycle drives further innovation and fuels their growth.

Ultimately, the role of innovation in modern startups cannot be underestimated. It is the driving force behind their success, enabling them to outperform their competitors and thrive in a rapidly changing business landscape. As the business world continues to evolve, innovation-driven startups will continue to lead the charge, shaping industries and creating new opportunities along the way.

## The Importance of Effective Communication in Startup Success

Effective communication is a vital component of startup success. It goes beyond exchanging information; it is the cornerstone of building strong relationships, fostering collaboration, and driving innovation within a startup environment.

*Deliberate communication* is key in startups, as it involves purposeful and intentional interactions. By clearly articulating goals, expectations, and ideas, startups can ensure that everyone is aligned and working towards a shared vision. Deliberate communication also minimizes misunderstandings and promotes efficiency.

Team collaboration is greatly enhanced by effective communication. When team members can openly express their thoughts, concerns, and ideas, it promotes a more inclusive and creative work atmosphere. Transparent leadership also plays a crucial role in facilitating communication within startups. Leaders who establish clear communication channels and foster an environment of openness and trust encourage team members to contribute their perspectives and insights.

*"Transparent leadership is paramount in startups. It creates an environment where team members feel safe to share ideas, ask questions, and raise concerns. By fostering transparency, startups can harness the collective intelligence of their team and empower individuals to take ownership of their work."*

Regular updates and progress reports are essential for effective communication in startups. These keep team members informed, provide clarity on objectives, and enable timely course corrections if needed. By sharing information openly, startups can foster a positive work culture and enhance team cohesion.

Effective communication also enables startups to overcome challenges more effectively. By openly discussing issues, sharing different perspectives, and seeking input from various stakeholders, startups can find innovative solutions and navigate obstacles with greater agility. It also helps prevent miscommunication or assumptions that can derail progress.

In conclusion, effective communication is a critical factor in the success of modern startups. Deliberate communication, team collaboration, and transparent leadership create a culture of trust, foster innovation, and promote problem-solving. By prioritizing effective communication, startups can build strong foundations for growth and navigate the complexities of the business landscape with confidence.

## Scaling Up: Navigating Growth in Modern Startups

Scaling up is a critical phase in the growth of modern startups. As these businesses expand, it becomes essential to implement effective scaling strategies that allow for manageable growth while maintaining operational efficiency. This requires careful planning, strategic decision-making, and a focus on maintaining the core values and culture that drove the startup's initial success.

One key aspect of scaling up is team expansion. Startups need to hire the right talent to support their growing operations and bring in expertise that aligns with their vision and objectives. By building a strong team, startups can distribute responsibilities, streamline processes, and enhance productivity. Effective team expansion helps ensure that the organization has the capacity to handle increased demand and deliver quality products or services.

*"As a startup scales, optimizing processes becomes crucial for maintaining operational efficiency. Startups must evaluate their existing workflows and identify areas where improvements can be made. By streamlining processes, eliminating bottlenecks, and implementing efficient systems, startups can effectively accommodate increased demand without sacrificing quality or customer satisfaction."*

Another critical aspect of scaling up is implementing scaling strategies that align with the startup's growth objectives. These strategies may include expanding into new markets, diversifying product or service offerings, or leveraging partnerships and collaborations. By strategically scaling the business, startups can capitalize on growth opportunities and position themselves for long-term success.

To navigate growth successfully, startups must also prioritize operational efficiency. By optimizing processes, utilizing technology, and leveraging data-driven insights, startups can maximize productivity and minimize waste. Operational efficiency not only helps startups streamline their operations but also enhances the overall customer experience, leading to increased customer satisfaction and loyalty.

## Ensuring a Successful Transition to Scale

As startups transition from early-stage to scale-up mode, it is important to approach growth with the right mindset and strategy. By implementing effective scaling strategies, expanding the team strategically, and maintaining operational efficiency, startups can navigate the challenges and opportunities that come with scaling up.

*"Scaling up is a journey that requires continuous learning, adaptability, and a willingness to embrace change. Successful startups understand the importance of maintaining agility and leveraging their core strengths as they grow. By remaining customer-focused, fostering innovation, and staying true to their values, startups can navigate the complexities of scaling up and position themselves for sustainable growth and long-term success."*

## The Future of Modern Startups: Embracing Uncertainty and Opportunity

In an ever-evolving business landscape, the future of startups hinges on their ability to adapt and embrace uncertainty. The traditional approach of rigid business models and long-term planning is gradually fading away, making room for startups that adopt an agile mindset. Startups that exhibit flexibility and adaptability will be better positioned to navigate the challenges and opportunities that lie ahead.

Embracing uncertainty opens doors to innovation and disruption. Startups that are willing to take risks, experiment with new ideas, and challenge the status quo are the ones that will shape the future of industries. By breaking free from conventional thinking and embracing uncertainty, startups can stay ahead of the curve and create a competitive edge.

The evolving business landscape offers a wealth of opportunities for startups. Emerging technologies, shifting consumer behaviors, and global socioeconomic changes open up new avenues for innovation and growth. By keeping a finger on the pulse of these trends, startups can identify emerging markets, develop innovative solutions, and position themselves as industry leaders.

To thrive in the future, startups must foster an agile mindset within their teams. This requires cultivating a culture of adaptability, open-mindedness, and continuous learning. The ability to quickly pivot, iterate, and respond to changing market dynamics will be crucial for staying relevant and seizing new opportunities.

Chapter 9

# Navigating the Growth Stage
## Introduction to the Growth Stage

In the ebb and flow of a company's lifecycle, the Growth Stage emerges as a particularly significant phase. This period is characterized by a dramatic surge in revenues and an increased share in the marketplace. However, just as a ship sailing into uncharted waters encounters unexpected currents, so too does a company venture into its growth stage grapple with unforeseen growth challenges.

During this transformative stage, businesses experience an influx of growth opportunities. On the one hand, there lies the potential for rapid expansion and scaling to greater heights; on the other hand, there remains the mountainous task of managing this newfound expansion and maintaining the quality standards that set the company apart in its infancy.

Growth for companies represents a double-edged sword where success is paired with increase in competition and operational complexities. These challenges tax companies at every turn, demanding effective management and strategic decisions to ensure stability amongst chaos. Indeed, navigating this tempestuous but rewarding stage requires astute understanding and immaculate planning.

The key to surviving the growth stage is not merely surviving it, but mastering it. To do so, businesses must understand exactly what this stage entails, what challenges lie ahead and prepare a strategic blueprint to navigate through these hurdles. This understanding comes from investigating concepts like "scaling operations", "maintaining quality", and "investing effectively" which are essential features of this stage.

A company's ability to transition smoothly into the growth stage largely depends on its core understanding of its operability during this time. It is crucial to grasp that scaling operations do not mean solely increasing production or services in response to growing market demand. Instead, it involves intricate processes aimed at expanding operational capability while preserving - or even improving - the quality of output.

Maintaining quality throughout this phase can seem like walking a tightrope. As companies scale up, they must find a balance between meeting increased market demand and maintaining their standing as a provider of quality products or services.

Investment, too, plays a critical role in a company's growth stage. Funds are required to fuel expansion and improve infrastructure, but the decision-making process can be rife with investment challenges. Investments during this stage must be astutely managed, taking into consideration several factors such as market volatility, competitors' strategies, supply chain management, and operational efficiencies.

In summary, successful navigation through the growth stage requires careful examination of both the opportunities presented and the corresponding challenges. It involves strategic maneuvers to scale operations while preserving product or service quality, and thoughtful investment decisions that support this process. Ensuring these components work together harmoniously is essential for businesses aiming to sail smoothly into the sunset of success.

## Understanding Middle-Aged Companies

In the hierarchical structure of the business ecosystem, middle-aged companies often find themselves in a unique yet challenging situation. Like adolescence in human life, this phase represents a company's transition from a budding start-up to a seasoned enterprise. This stage is rife with opportunities, but it also brings along its fair share of obstacles and middle-aged company challenges.

The hallmark feature of middle-aged companies is their dire need for expansion - be it in terms of market reach, production capacity or workforce strength. Add to this the pressing requirement to maintain high-quality standards, and these enterprises face what seems like an uphill task. The scaling challenge thus becomes one of primary concern at this point.

A common pitfall for many businesses in their middle age is naively equating scaling with uncontrolled growth. However, true scalability involves careful planning and systematic execution that ensures sustainable growth across all dimensions without causing compromise on product quality or service delivery. "Scaling operations" therefore doesn't merely imply increasing output but encompasses streamlining processes, optimizing resources utilization and boosting productivity while maintaining high quality standards.

In tandem with scaling efforts, another formidable challenge that middle-aged companies often encounter is the constant pressure to evolve and adapt. This can involve anything from responding to emerging trends within the industry to adopting new technological advancements; all while keeping an eye on the competition and ensuring customer satisfaction remains uncompromised. The weighty responsibility of quality maintenance, then, extends beyond managing resources and workflows; it necessitates staying abreast with dynamic market environments and tailoring strategies accordingly.

Coupled with these operational hurdles, there are financial barriers to consider too. On one hand, any effort at growth demands substantial funding and therefore managing investments becomes a crucial task. On the other hand, middle-aged companies are often met with constraints in soliciting external capital due to the higher risks associated with scaling operations and venturing into new territories.

These investment challenges can manifest themselves in several ways - from securing sufficient funds for expansion, to managing cash flow while investing in new markets or technologies. The necessity of maintaining profitability during this period adds to these financial complexities.

In essence, understanding middle-aged companies is akin to peering into a nuanced kaleidoscope of challenges. From operational dilemmas like scaling and quality maintenance, to fiscal struggles tied to investment management; each layer brings its own set of hurdles. However, it's important to remember that these obstacles aren't insurmountable roadblocks but stepping stones that pave the path for growth if navigated astutely. After all, successful businesses aren't those which avoid challenges, but those which embrace them as opportunities for improvement and innovation.

**Scaling Operations While Maintaining Quality**

As companies journey through their middle age, one of the primary challenges they grapple with is scaling operations while preserving product or service quality. The underpinning principle of scaling operations isn't about merely fueling numeric growth - producing more goods or offering more services, but facilitating sustainable and efficient growth.

Imagine a tree growing in fast-forward. If it only grows upwards without providing equal attention to its roots, it is bound to topple over, unable to support itself. This analogy perfectly captures the predicament of middle-aged companies aiming for rapid scaling without establishing a solid framework. As these enterprises try to grow at an exponential rate, they risk neglecting the essential components that hold up the entire business architecture - the quality of their offerings.

Maintaining quality during this expansion phase is often likened to walking a thin tightrope - one misstep can lead to catastrophic fallouts. The key lies in integrating 'quality control' into every aspect of your scaling strategy, from workforce expansion to the adoption of new technologies. It's imperative to remember that quality isn't just confined to products or services delivered; it permeates various other aspects including customer service, internal processes, supplier relationships and beyond.

Quality assurance should be woven into even the minutest details of operational expansion – ensuring new hires align with company culture and values, streamlining communication protocols as teams grow and become more dispersed, guaranteeing reliable supply chains amid increased production demand. Ensuring high-quality standards amidst growth is not something that happens by coincidence but is an ongoing commitment to systematic planning, diligent execution, and meticulous review.

During this growth-scale juggle, technology often emerges as both a facilitator and disrupter. Rapid advancements in technology offer a wide array of tools that can increase efficiency and productivity. However, the misuse or over-reliance on technology can cause quality deterioration. Hence, in the scaling journey, it's important to carefully evaluate and adopt technologies that align with your business model and enhance your ability to deliver consistent quality.

Innovation plays a vital role when scaling operations while maintaining quality. Innovation doesn't necessarily refer to groundbreaking product developments but includes incremental improvements in processes or services that enhance overall experience and satisfaction for customers. Such innovations not only optimise operational efficiency but also help in retaining the company's competitive edge.

Lastly, creating a customer-centric culture is essential during this period. The voice of your customers is an invaluable guide that can steer you through the maze of growth-stage challenges. Feedback-driven improvements and adaptations help ensure that your scaling efforts do not drift away from what matters most - delivering quality products or services that meet or exceed customer expectations.

To sum up, managing the balancing act of growth and quality requires strategic planning, investment in right resources, embracing relevant technological solutions, fostering innovation and staying true to customer needs. It's about expanding capacity without losing sight of core values and commitments towards quality. Remember - scaling isn't just about growing big; it's about growing strong as well.

**The Art of Strategic Pivots and Its Impacts on Investment**

It is an undisputed truth that the only constant in the business world is change itself. Companies that thrive are those who are fluid enough to adapt their strategies and operations to align with these incessant shifts. This adaptation is often achieved through strategic pivots, a commonly employed yet frequently misunderstood maneuver within the growth-stage narrative.

A strategic pivot does not signify a failure or a sign of defeat; rather, it is an indication of awareness and agility. It signals a company's ability to recognize shifting trends, market demand, or competitive landscapes, subsequently making purposeful changes to capture valuable opportunities for growth. These agile maneuvers do not come without challenges and can significantly impact investment decisions during this pivotal stage.

Whether it's shifting from one product line to another that's experiencing massive demand or responding to technological advancements by overhauling traditional operational processes, pivots require careful thought, impeccable timing, and significant capital inputs. Consequently, they pose both investment challenges and opportunities.

The decision to pivot invariably involves elements of risks and uncertainties. Investing in a new direction necessitates thorough evaluation of potential returns against associated risks. It requires extensive research into market trends, competitor positioning, customer preferences and economic forecasts. Stakeholders may feel ambivalent about such changes - while some view them as necessary for survival and progression, others might see them as risky endeavors that could dilute the original mission and vision of the company.

Balancing these contrasting viewpoints often poses as a challenge for businesses seeking investments during their pivot phase. Navigating these waters requires not just flexibility but also strong leadership, effective communication about the changing course, clear understanding of the pivot's potential impacts on the company's financial health and future growth prospects, and utmost transparency in dealing with stakeholders.

While the strategic pivot can create some initial disruption, it often opens doors to new investment opportunities. It signals to investors that a company is proactive, highly adaptable, and poised for growth, even in a volatile business environment. This adaptability and forward-thinking approach can make the firm more attractive to prospective investors, who appreciate enterprises that aren't just reactive but are strategically proactive.

In conclusion, understanding the art of strategic pivots and their influence on investment ventures is an integral part of growth-stage navigation. With proper planning, careful execution, and transparent communication, these maneuvers can act as a momentum shifter that steers businesses through middle-aged challenges toward success. The key lies in remembering that each pivot is a stepping stone towards resilience and not simply a reaction to adversity. It's about steering the ship carefully through stormy seas rather than waiting passively for the storm to pass.

## Case Studies Analysis

To contextualize the theoretical understanding of growth stage survival, it is worthwhile to observe the real-world implications through some compelling case studies. Analyzing these instances enables us to capture the essence of strategic pivots, scaling operations, maintaining quality and battling investment challenges during a company's mid-life journey.

Consider Netflix, a classic example of strategic pivoting in action. Netflix began its journey as a DVD-by-mail service but soon recognized the potential of streaming technology. Their pivotal move is now considered a masterstroke as they transitioned from their traditional model to successfully dominating the online streaming market. Here, the keyword is 'successfully.' Netflix didn't just pivot; they ensured that this shift was underpinned by diligent planning and execution which preserved their brand value while scaling operations remarkably.

Nike, known worldwide for its sportswear products, also provides an excellent insight into managing quality while scaling operations. Over years, Nike has grown enormously, yet it has not compromised on its product quality at any point. Its commitment to consistent high-quality products coupled with innovative strategy has resulted in customer loyalty and business sustainability.

However, not all middle-aged companies witness success stories. Case in point: Kodak. Once a pioneer in photography technology, Kodak struggled to innovate and adapt to digital photography trends. This inability to pivot strategically ultimately led to its downfall, offering key lessons on embracing change.

Digging into such stories offers valuable insights into what works – and what doesn't – for middle-aged companies looking to navigate growth challenges effectively. It demonstrates how strategic decisions can foster or inhibit scalability and affect overall investment plans.

Furthermore, scouring business news sources can reveal myriad instances reflecting similar scenarios across various sectors - be it clothing giants scaling their operations globally, tech firms pivoting to stay relevant in the evolving digital landscape, or startups grappling with investment woes. It's essential to pay attention to such narratives as they provide practical perspectives on theoretical concepts.

Whether it is a story of victory or a tale of struggle, each case study provides a priceless lesson. These real-world instances are like signposts on the journey, offering clear indications of the potential obstacles and possible solutions. They serve as practical guides that can inform strategic decisions, both big and small, encountered during the growth stage.

Through these case studies, industry news reports and stories of other businesses at a similar stage, middle-aged companies can equip themselves with actionable insights, better prepare for what lies ahead and empower themselves to navigate through growth-stage challenges successfully.

# Chapter 10

# The Equity Story

- Equity distribution and its importance
- Employee stock options and investor shares
- Managing cap tables effectively

# Exit Strategies

## An Introduction to Successful Exit Strategies

When it comes to business, strategizing is crucial for success. This remains true even when planning for an exit. What are exit strategies, you may ask? Simply put, an *exit strategy* is a plan a business entrepreneur formulates to sell their ownership in a company and exit with maximum profitability. The term *"Chapter 11"* often echoes in this realm of discussion as it is a commonly used exit strategy.

## The Landscape of Exit Strategies

*Understanding the exit landscape* is the first step towards formulating a successful exit strategy. It involves examining various means by which an entrepreneur can make a profitable exit from their company. These include methods such as Initial Public Offerings (IPOs), acquisitions, and buyouts.

## Initial Public Offerings (IPOs)

An IPO is an instance where a private corporation goes public by selling its stocks to general investors. It's a viable way for companies to raise capital while providing returns to its initial backers.

## Acquisitions

Acquisitions involve another company buying the major stake in your enterprise. Generally, this is considered when the acquirer company wishes to expand its market reach or attain new technologies.

## Buyouts

A buyout usually happens when investors, often in private equity firms, buy the majority of a company's shares thereby gaining control over its operations and decisions.

## Strategizing Your Company's Successful Exit

Real-life cases further illustrate these paths. For instance, Facebook's acquisition of Instagram and WhatsApp showcases a successful corporate acquisition strategy. Similarly, the IPO of giants like Google and Alibaba demonstrate how going public can lead to enormous gains for early backers.

Exit strategies are an important part of entrepreneurial ventures. They're not designed out of pessimism; rather, they're drawn up with the aim of facilitating a fruitful culmination to a successful enterprise. The right exit strategy can ensure maximum returns for founders and investors alike. Understanding the concept of *"Chapter 11: Crafting Successful Exit Strategies"* is crucial in maneuvering this complex landscape towards an optimal entrepreneurial exit.

## Diving Deeper into IPOs, Acquisitions, and Buyouts

Having a basic understanding of exit strategies such as Initial Public Offerings (IPOs), acquisitions, and buyouts is just the tip of the iceberg. To truly benefit from these strategies, it's vital that companies are well-equipped with profound knowledge of each option – ensuring *IPO readiness*, conducting smooth transactions during an acquisition or buyout, and more.

## Initial Public Offerings (IPOs): A Gateway to Going Public

When a private company decides to go public via an IPO, there's a flurry of preparation involved. Private companies must gear up for *going public*, which involves thorough auditing, compiling financial statements, filing registration documents with relevant authorities, and setting the price band for stocks. The journey from being a private entity to stepping into the open market place can be complex, but the rewards can be substantial.

In terms of *IPO readiness*, it's essential to build an experienced team of advisors including lawyers, accountants, and underwriters to help navigate this intricate process. Your roadmap for an IPO should include analyzing market conditions for optimal timing, preparing your firm's corporate structure and governance protocols fit for public scrutiny, and developing comprehensive investor relations strategies to attract potential shareholders.

## Acquisitions: An Organized Shift of Power

An acquisition deal isn't simply about handing over the majority stake in your company—it involves careful planning too. To prepare for a potentially *successful exit* via an acquisition, ensure all your legal paperwork is in order. This would include licenses, contracts with clients or vendors, employment agreements among others. Additionally, having an accurate valuation of your business and understanding the tax consequences of an acquisition deal are critical elements for a profitable exit.

## Buyouts: An Investor's Path to Control

A buyout strategy essentially involves one or more investors buying out the controlling stake in a company. It's a popular choice for private equity firms, as it often provides them with direct control over their investment. For businesses, this exit strategy can serve as a robust funding mechanism, particularly when preparing for expansion or restructuring.

Executing successful *buyouts* usually requires careful assessment of fair value of the company by potential buyers. Equally important is demonstrating a promising vision for future growth and profitability of the business under new ownership. Working closely with financial advisors to craft a compelling narrative around these aspects can significantly enhance the chances of securing a lucrative agreement.

In conclusion, IPOs, acquisitions, and buyouts each have their unique sets of requirements and advantages. As such, companies must prepare according to the specific exit strategy they choose to follow. Arming oneself with detailed knowledge about each tactic is key when it comes to maximizing profits from these strategic moves.

## Successful Company Exits and Lessons Learned

Having reviewed the mechanism of various exit strategies, in this segment, let's dive deeper into successful real-life instances and draw key lessons from them. Observing these strategies in action across diverse industries can help us understand how to *prepare a company for a successful exit.*

## A Glance at the Greatest IPOs: Facebook and Alibaba

Undoubtedly among the most noteworthy IPOs in history include those of tech giants Facebook and Alibaba. In 2012, *Facebook went public* raising $16 billion, making it one of the largest tech IPOs in U.S history. However, as a lesson for budding entrepreneurs, its immediate post-IPO performance was riddled with technical issues and litigation surrounding disclosure of revenue forecasts.

*Alibaba's IPO*, on the other hand, emerged as the largest offering globally when it raised $25 billion on New York Stock Exchange in 2014. An important takeaway here is their strategy of exposing its business operations to investors well ahead of time. This built investor confidence leading to an oversubscription of shares.

## The Acquisitive Google: Acquisition Pioneer

*Google's acquisition strategy*, particularly in its early years, set a precedent for startups contemplating exits via acquisitions. They have acquired a range of companies – large and small – including Android, YouTube, and Waze. Their acquisitions allowed them to diversify their portfolio rapidly while enabling brilliant returns for the owners of these fledgling firms. Their strategy offers critical insights on assessing your business's unique value proposition that would attract potential acquirers.

**Epic Buyouts: TXU and RJR Nabisco**

When talking about *buyouts,* two case studies stand out—the acquisition of TXU, a Texas-based energy company, and the buyout of RJR Nabisco by KKR. With $44 billion in 2007, TXU's buyout was led by private equity giants and is among the largest private equity buyouts to date. It underlines how buyouts can lead to strategic overhauls to drive future growth and profitability.

RJR Nabisco's leveraged buyout in 1988 for $31.4 billion painted a stark image of how aggressive leadership combined with high leverage could command such enormous deals. While initially successful, the long-term consequences of debt accumulation offer a cautionary tale for businesses considering high-leverage exits.

In Summary

The road to an exit strategy is paved with due diligence, intense preparation, and constant learning from successful (and unsuccessful) precedents. Whether it be through IPOs, acquisitions or buyouts, one must remember that at the core of every successful business exit lies tenacious leadership coupled with a thorough understanding of exit landscape.

**Preparing Your Company For a Successful Exit**

The ultimate objective of any good exit strategy is to ensure a profitable and smooth transition. However, achieving this requires thoughtful preparation, meticulous planning, and careful execution. From getting your financial records in order to developing a strong management team and understanding the complexities of *venture capital terms*, proactive steps taken today can significantly enhance your company's readiness for a successful exit.

**Understanding Your Company's Financial Health**

Your company's financial health is among the first things potential buyers or investors will look at. Make sure your financial statements are clear, comprehensive, and professionally audited. Understand and highlight key performance indicators that accurately reflect your company's value. Be transparent about debts, assets, revenues, profit margins, cash flow, among others – ambiguity or misrepresentation can lead to distrust or falling apart of potential deals.

**Familiarizing with Venture Capital Terms**

If you've sought venture capital (VC) investment in your company at any stage of its growth cycle, it's crucial to understand how those investments could impact an exit strategy. Understanding common *venture capital terms*, such as liquidation preference, participation rights and anti-dilution provisions can help you navigate these complexities during the negotiation process. They can also help minimize surprises once an exit opportunity arises.

**Cultivating Strong Leadership**

Exits often involve transitions - potentially even shifts in leadership roles. Therefore, having a strong middle-management tier can assure potential buyers that business operations will continue smoothly post-exit. Be proactive in grooming capable successors as part of your exit strategy - potential investors or buyers will see this as a sign that the company will continue to function well beyond its current leaders.

**Operational Efficiency**

Your company's operational efficiency manifests not just in how it functions, but also in how well it can maximize profits while minimizing resource utilization. Demonstrating such proficiency could significantly increase the value of your business to a prospective buyer or investor. Ensure that all operations - from logistics and supply chain management to customer service, are running efficiently and flawlessly.

**Legal Compliance**

It's important that you stay on top of legal matters related to your company. From regulatory compliance to contract and employment law, ensuring your business is legally sound is non-negotiable. It reduces risks associated with potential lawsuits or disputes that might devalue your business during the exit process.

## Investing in Private Equity

*Private equity* can play a crucial role in preparing for a successful exit. If done right, private equity investments can yield significant returns for businesses. *Private equity outlook* knowledge will equip entrepreneurs with the necessary financial acumen to steer their company towards success during an exit scenario. Additionally, getting involved in private equity provides access to a broader network of industry contacts which can add an intangible but critical value to your enterprise.

In conclusion, meticulous planning and strategic execution can lead you down the path of a successful exit. By taking these steps diligently, you are setting yourself up for enhanced control over the timing and terms of your eventual exit - ensuring a favorable outcome for all stakeholders involved.

## Understanding the Role of Private Equity in Exit Strategies

In conversations about exit strategies, *private equity* frequently takes center stage. Its significance and potential impact on successful exits cannot be understated. As we delve into the world of private equity, it's clear why this form of investment is often regarded as a game-changer for companies contemplating an exit.

## The Power of Private Equity

Private equity essentially involves investing funds directly into private companies or conducting buyouts of public firms resulting in their delisting from public exchanges. The end goal? To streamline operations, boost profitability, and ultimately sell the company at a higher price – either to other businesses or back to the public markets through an IPO.

The *strategic exit strategy* offered by private equity investments often packs immense potential for a lucrative exit. It allows companies to tap into substantial capital infusion that can drive growth while simultaneously creating an avenue for eventual profitable exit through a sale or a buyout.

## Benefits of Private Equity Investments

Beyond injecting capital, private equity investments come with numerous benefits. Professional PE firms bring aboard industry expertise that can help shape strategic direction, financial acumen for more informed decision-making, operational know-how for efficiency improvements and importantly—a network of valuable contacts that could further fuel growth. The prevalence and success of *"retail's largest private equity buyouts"* are testament to how this route can not only drive business growth but also pave the way for lucrative exit strategies.

## A Closer Look At Private Equity Buyouts

Buyouts have become a common fixture in the private equity landscape. In essence, they involve acquisition of controlling interest in a company's equity, often with the goal of taking over its management and operation. But why are PE buyouts often linked with successful exits? The answer lies in *"private equity outlook"* and strategic focus. Post-acquisition, the private equity firm works on improving operational efficiencies and bottom-line results to enhance the valuation of their portfolio companies over time. This better positions them for a profitable exit through subsequent sale or an IPO.

## How to Prepare for Private Equity Investment

Attracting private equity investment necessitates careful preparation. Understanding your business's worth is fundamental. A comprehensive valuation analysis can provide an accurate picture of your firm's wealth and demonstrate its value to potential investors. Develop a solid business plan showcasing future growth prospects as that is what investors will bank on for their returns.

Sound financial management is critical - regular audits, clean tax records, efficient cash-flow management, and steady revenue streams stand you in good stead. Also, ensure that your legal house is in order—legal compliance, transparent contracts and agreements are crucial in instilling investor confidence.

Including private equity in your exit strategy matrix opens up a realm of possibilities but does require strategic planning and execution. Businesses that effectively leverage this avenue stand poised not only to unlock substantial growth opportunities but also potentially achieve successful exits.

# The Role of Advisory Boards

Welcome to Chapter 12. In this chapter, we delve into the vital role of advisory boards and their impact on driving business growth and securing funding. Advisory boards are a valuable resource for entrepreneurs, offering insights and guidance to navigate the complexities of running a business.

Entrepreneurs often face challenges in developing effective business strategies, but advisory boards can provide valuable expertise and industry knowledge to help shape these strategies. With their guidance, entrepreneurs can identify growth opportunities, mitigate risks, and make informed decisions to propel their businesses forward. Furthermore, advisory boards play a crucial role in securing funding, leveraging their networks to connect entrepreneurs with potential investors.

In this chapter, we explore the benefits of assembling an effective advisory board, the differences between advisory boards and boards of directors, and the roles and responsibilities of advisory board members. We'll also discuss best practices for selecting and recruiting advisory board members, the function of advisory boards in business strategy, and their impact on accessing funding. Additionally, we'll cover how leveraging the networks of advisory board members can open doors to new partnerships and collaborations.

Effective advisory board meetings and evaluating the board's success are essential aspects we'll explore. We'll also address the challenges and pitfalls that entrepreneurs might encounter when working with advisory boards.

By the end of this chapter, you'll have a comprehensive understanding of how advisory boards contribute to the success of businesses. So let's dive in and discover how advisory boards can benefit your business strategy, drive growth, and secure funding!

## The Benefits of Advisory Boards

Assembling an effective advisory board can bring numerous benefits to a business. Advisors can provide valuable expertise, industry knowledge, and connections that can help entrepreneurs secure funding and identify growth opportunities. By leveraging their networks, advisors can open doors to new partnerships and collaborations.

*Having an advisory board is like having a team of trusted advisors who can guide you through the challenges and complexities of running a business. These individuals bring a wealth of experience and diverse perspectives to the table, offering valuable insights that can shape strategic decisions and drive growth.*

One of the key benefits of assembling an advisory board is their ability to assist in securing funding. Advisors with industry connections and a strong network can introduce entrepreneurs to potential investors, increasing the chances of securing crucial funding for business ventures. Furthermore, advisory board members often have extensive knowledge of the market and industry trends. Their insights can help entrepreneurs identify new growth opportunities and stay ahead of the competition. By leveraging the expertise of advisory board members, businesses can make informed decisions that contribute to long-term success.

## The Power of Networks

Advisory board members not only bring their individual expertise, but they also offer access to their networks. By leveraging the networks of advisory board members, businesses can forge new partnerships, collaborations, and strategic alliances. This access to a broader network can open up new avenues for growth and expansion.

For example, consider a tech startup looking to enter a new market. An advisory board member who has connections in that market can provide introductions to key players, potential customers, and distribution channels. These connections can significantly accelerate the startup's market entry and support business growth.

In summary, assembling an effective advisory board can provide a business with invaluable expertise, industry insights, and access to networks that can help secure funding, identify growth opportunities, and drive long-term success. Entrepreneurs should carefully consider the expertise and connections they need and select advisory board members who align with their business goals and values.

## Advisory Boards vs. Boards of Directors

When it comes to decision-making in a business, it's important to understand the distinction between advisory boards and boards of directors. While both play crucial roles in steering the direction of a company, they operate in different capacities.

Boards of directors are the governing bodies with legal authority and responsibility for making binding decisions that impact the business. They are typically composed of high-ranking executives and industry experts who have the power to shape company policies, make important strategic decisions, and oversee the overall operations of the organization.

On the other hand, advisory boards offer non-binding strategic advice to the business. They are composed of industry professionals, experts, and influencers who provide valuable insights and guidance based on their expertise and experience. Advisory boards act as a sounding board for entrepreneurs, offering fresh perspectives, unbiased opinions, and valuable insights without taking on the legal responsibilities of a board of directors.

Advisory boards can be immensely beneficial to businesses in many ways. They bring diverse perspectives, industry knowledge, and valuable contacts. Entrepreneurs can leverage their advisory board members' expertise to gain a competitive advantage, make informed decisions, and identify growth opportunities.

*"The role of an advisory board is to support and help companies navigate challenges, identify opportunities, and maximize their potential. Their non-binding advice enables businesses to benefit from the expertise and networks of these respected industry leaders."*

By engaging with advisory boards, entrepreneurs can tap into a pool of talented advisors who can offer independent advice, challenge assumptions, and provide valuable insights. The diverse perspectives of advisory board members can contribute to well-rounded decision-making and help businesses adapt to changing market dynamics.

While boards of directors have the final say in decision-making, advisory boards act as a valuable resource, assisting and supplementing the decision-making process. They can provide the necessary guidance and expertise to help entrepreneurs make informed choices that align with their business goals and strategic vision.

In summary, while boards of directors hold decision-making authority, advisory boards offer non-binding strategic advice, fresh perspectives, unbiased opinions, and valuable insights. The incorporation of both boards allows businesses to benefit from legal accountability and expert advice, driving growth and success.

| Advisory Boards | Boards of Directors |
|---|---|
| Provide non-binding strategic advice | Make binding decisions |
| Offer fresh perspectives and unbiased opinions | Have the legal responsibility for decision-making |
| Bring industry expertise and valuable contacts | Oversee the overall operations of the organization |

**Roles and Responsibilities of Advisory Board Members**

Advisory board members play a critical role in the success of an organization, bringing their expertise, experience, and industry knowledge to the table. They have specific responsibilities within the organization and serve as valuable resources for entrepreneurs and business leaders. Their primary roles include:

1. *Offering Feedback and Advice:* Advisory board members act as sounding boards, providing valuable feedback and advice on business decisions, strategic direction, and market trends. Their input helps entrepreneurs make informed decisions that contribute to the overall growth and success of the business. They bring fresh perspectives and insights, challenging conventional thinking and encouraging innovation.

2. *Providing Expertise:* Advisory board members bring a wealth of expertise in their respective fields. They contribute their industry knowledge, skills, and networks to support the organization's goals and initiatives. Their diverse backgrounds and experiences can help businesses navigate industry challenges, identify growth opportunities, and stay competitive.

3. *Guiding Strategic Direction:* Advisory board members play a key role in shaping the strategic direction of the organization. They provide guidance on long-term goals, help identify potential risks, and suggest strategies to optimize business performance. By leveraging their collective knowledge and insights, advisory board members assist in developing actionable plans that align with the organization's vision and mission.

*"Having the right advisory board members can truly make a difference in building a successful business. Their valuable feedback and advice, coupled with their industry expertise, contribute to strategic decision-making and overall organizational growth."*

Overall, advisory board members collaborate with entrepreneurs and business leaders to drive forward-thinking strategies, encourage innovation, and promote long-term sustainability. Their active engagement and commitment are essential for maximizing the potential of advisory boards in achieving organizational goals.

| Role | Responsibilities |
|------|------------------|
| Offering Feedback and Advice | Act as sounding boards for business decisions, strategic direction, and market trends. Provide valuable feedback and offer advice. |
| Providing Expertise | Contribute industry knowledge, skills, and networks to support organizational goals. Help navigate challenges and identify growth opportunities. |
| Guiding Strategic Direction | Shape the strategic direction of the organization. Provide guidance on long-term goals, risk management, and performance optimization. |

**Selecting and Recruiting Advisory Board Members**

When it comes to selecting and recruiting advisory board members, entrepreneurs should approach the process with careful consideration. Building a well-rounded advisory board can provide valuable expertise and diverse perspectives, helping drive business growth and success. To ensure a successful selection, entrepreneurs should focus on individuals with relevant industry experience, a wide range of skill sets, and a genuine passion for the business.

*"A well-constructed advisory board can offer invaluable advice and guidance to businesses,"* *says John Smith, a business consultant with years of experience. "By selecting board members who bring diverse backgrounds and insights, entrepreneurs can access a wealth of knowledge that can fuel innovation and strategic decision-making."*

When recruiting advisors, entrepreneurs should consider individuals with deep industry knowledge and a track record of success. This expertise can help businesses navigate challenges and identify new opportunities for growth. By recruiting board members who are passionate about the business and its mission, entrepreneurs can foster a strong sense of commitment and dedication.

The recruitment process should involve a thoughtful evaluation of each potential advisory board member's qualifications and alignment with the business's needs. Entrepreneurs can conduct interviews, request references, and review candidates' past experiences to assess their suitability. The goal is to assemble a board that complements the entrepreneur's skills and fills any knowledge gaps.

### Building a Well-Rounded Advisory Board

An effective advisory board consists of individuals who bring diverse expertise and perspectives to the table. By assembling a well-rounded board, entrepreneurs can access a wide range of knowledge and insights. It is important to include members with different backgrounds, specialties, and industry connections.

"Diversity is key," says Jane Johnson, an entrepreneur who successfully built an advisory board for her tech startup. "Having a mix of experiences and skill sets on the board ensures that you receive well-rounded advice from people who can look at the business challenges from various angles."

**The table below showcases the importance of diversity in selecting advisory board members:**

| Skills | Industry Experience | Network | Passion for the Business |
|---|---|---|---|
| Strategic Planning | Technology | Venture Capital | Entrepreneurial mindset |
| Financial Management | Finance | Industry Associations | Commitment to innovation |
| Marketing and Sales | Marketing | Business Development | Understanding of target market |
| Operational Efficiency | Operations | Supply Chain | Shared purpose and values |

The table above highlights the importance of selecting advisory board members with diverse skills, experience, and networks. By assembling a board that covers a broad spectrum of expertise, entrepreneurs can benefit from a multifaceted approach to decision-making and problem-solving.

By selecting and recruiting advisory board members with care, entrepreneurs can ensure that their board provides them with the guidance and support they need to navigate the complexities of running a successful business.

### The Function of Advisory Boards in Business Strategy

Advisory boards play a vital role in shaping and refining business strategy. Their valuable input during strategic planning sessions can help entrepreneurs identify opportunities, mitigate risks, and make informed decisions. By leveraging the expertise and insights of advisory board members, businesses can achieve long-term growth and success.

*"Advisory boards bring a fresh perspective and unique insights that can significantly impact the strategic direction of a business."*

During strategic planning, advisory board members contribute their industry knowledge, experience, and diverse perspectives. This collaborative effort ensures that the business strategy aligns with market trends, customer needs, and the company's overall vision. The advisory board's input enables entrepreneurs to make well-informed decisions based on a holistic understanding of the business landscape.

Strategic planning sessions with the advisory board allow for critical discussions, brainstorming, and evaluation of potential opportunities and challenges. By involving advisory board members, businesses can tap into a wealth of knowledge and expertise, providing a solid foundation for informed decision-making.

*"Strategic planning sessions with the advisory board provide a valuable opportunity to tap into varied perspectives, challenge assumptions, and explore new growth avenues."*

The function of advisory boards in business strategy can range from offering insights on market trends, competitive analysis, and customer behavior to providing feedback on product development, pricing strategies, and expansion plans. Advisory board members contribute their expertise to help businesses chart a course for success.

With their breadth of knowledge, advisory boards can bring fresh ideas, innovative solutions, and alternative approaches to strategic planning. Their inputs can spark creativity, encourage out-of-the-box thinking, and help businesses stay ahead in a competitive landscape.

Integrating Advisory Board Recommendations into Business Strategy

Once strategic planning sessions conclude, it's crucial for entrepreneurs to integrate advisory board recommendations into their business strategy effectively. Clear action plans, assigned responsibilities, and regular communication facilitate the successful implementation of advisory board insights.

*"Integrating advisory board recommendations requires a collaborative approach and effective communication channels between the board, management, and key stakeholders."*

By aligning the strategic objectives with the feedback and recommendations received from the advisory board, businesses can maximize the impact of their collaborative efforts. Regular follow-ups and progress updates ensure that the business strategy remains dynamic and adaptable to evolving market conditions.

Throughout the entire process, entrepreneurs should foster an open and trusting relationship with advisory board members. Mutual respect, effective communication, and a shared vision of success are essential for leveraging the full potential of the advisory board in shaping and refining business strategy.

**Benefits of Advisory Boards in Business Strategy**

The involvement of advisory boards in strategic planning offers numerous benefits to businesses:

| Benefits | Explanation |
| --- | --- |
| External Perspective | Advisory board members bring fresh ideas and diverse perspectives, challenging internal assumptions and promoting innovative thinking. |
| Industry Expertise | Advisory board members possess extensive industry knowledge and experience, enabling them to provide valuable insights and recommendations specific to the business's context. |
| Reduced Bias | Advisory boards offer an impartial and objective viewpoint, ensuring that decisions are not influenced solely by internal stakeholders or personal agendas. |
| Network Access | Advisory board members often have broad networks with influential individuals and strategic partners, providing valuable connections for business development and growth opportunities. |
| Mitigating Risks | Advisory boards help businesses identify potential risks, evaluate their impact, and develop strategies to minimize or overcome them. |

**Advisory Boards and Funding**

Advisory boards can play a crucial role in helping businesses secure the funding they need to thrive. With their extensive industry connections and expertise, advisory board members can guide entrepreneurs through the complex process of navigating the investment landscape and attracting potential investors.

By leveraging their network, advisors can open doors to new funding opportunities and introductions to key stakeholders. Their insights and recommendations can significantly improve the chances of securing crucial funding for business ventures.

*"Our advisory board played a vital role in securing the funding we needed to take our business to the next level. Their connections and expertise gave us a massive advantage in attracting investors and getting the support we needed to grow." Janet Asquith CEO*

Advisory board members bring a wealth of industry knowledge and experience to the table, allowing entrepreneurs to tap into their expertise during fundraising efforts. Their insights can help refine business strategies, fine-tune pitches, and identify key investment opportunities.

Furthermore, advisory boards can offer valuable guidance in terms of investment readiness, providing entrepreneurs with the necessary feedback and recommendations to make their business attractive to potential investors.

## Leveraging Advisory Board Insights for Securing Investment

Advisory boards provide a unique perspective and valuable insights that can improve the chances of securing investment. Here are some ways advisory board members can contribute to the funding process:

Ways Advisory Board Members Can Help Secure Investment

1. Introductions to key investors and venture capitalists

2. Guidance in refining business plans and investment strategies

3. Assistance in developing compelling pitches and presentations

4. Insights on current market trends and investor expectations

5. Validation of business models and growth potential

With their support, entrepreneurs can seamlessly navigate the funding landscape, optimize their fundraising efforts, and increase their chances of securing the investment needed to fuel business growth.

## Advisory Boards and Network Leveraging

Leveraging the networks of advisory board members is a powerful strategy for businesses seeking growth and expansion. With their extensive connections across various industries, advisors can open doors to opportunities, resources, partnerships, and collaborations that can fuel business growth.

*"The networks of advisory board members can be an invaluable asset for entrepreneurs,"* says John Smith, CEO of ABC Corporation. *"By tapping into their connections, businesses can gain access to new markets, customers, and potential investors."*

Advisory board members, being seasoned professionals in their respective fields, have built strong relationships over the years. These relationships can serve as valuable conduits for businesses looking to grow and acquire new customers or partners. Through their networks, advisors can introduce entrepreneurs to key stakeholders, strategic partners, and potential clients.

Harnessing the power of advisory board networks not only accelerates business growth but also enhances the reputation and credibility of the company. By associating with well-connected advisors, businesses gain a stamp of approval that can attract more customers, investors, and potential business partners.

To illustrate the impact of network leveraging, consider the table below showcasing the growth achieved by a business with an advisory board compared to a business without one:

|  | Business A (With Advisory Board) | Business B (Without Advisory Board) |
| --- | --- | --- |
| Annual Revenue Growth | 30% | 12% |
| Partnerships Established | 10 | 3 |
| New Market Entry | 2 | 0 |

As evidenced by the table, advisory boards can significantly contribute to business growth. The business with an advisory board (Business A) experienced higher revenue growth, established more partnerships, and successfully entered new markets compared to the business without an advisory board (Business B).

By leveraging the networks of advisory board members, businesses can position themselves for success, accessing a wealth of opportunities that would otherwise be out of reach. Having advisors with diverse connections and industry expertise is essential for maximizing the benefits of network leveraging and driving sustainable business growth.

**Best Practices for Advisory Board Meetings**

Running effective advisory board meetings is crucial to maximize the benefits of the board and obtain valuable insights from advisory board members. By following these best practices, entrepreneurs can ensure productive and collaborative meetings that drive business growth.

*1. Establish Clear Meeting Objectives:* Before each meeting, clearly define the objectives and desired outcomes. This helps focus the discussion and ensures that all attendees are aligned and prepared for the meeting agenda.

*2. Provide Relevant Materials in Advance:* Distribute necessary documents, reports, or presentations to advisory board members at least a few days before the meeting. This allows them ample time to review the materials and come prepared with insightful feedback and recommendations.

*3. Foster an Open and Collaborative Environment:* Create an atmosphere that encourages open and honest conversations. Establishing trust between the entrepreneur and advisory board members promotes a free exchange of ideas and diverse perspectives, leading to more valuable insights and strategic guidance.

*4. Encourage Active Participation:* Encourage all advisory board members to actively participate in the discussions and contribute their expertise. Keep the meeting format inclusive, allowing everyone to voice their opinions and ask questions when necessary.

*5. Allocate Time for Q&A and Discussion:* Set aside dedicated time for questions, clarifications, and detailed discussions. This allows advisory board members to delve deeper into specific topics, share their insights, and provide valuable input on critical business decisions.

*6. Take Meeting Minutes:* Assign someone to take comprehensive meeting minutes that document key decisions, action items, and recommendations. These minutes serve as a valuable reference for future meetings and ensure accountability for implementing follow-up actions.

*7. Regular Communication and Follow-Up:* Maintain regular communication with advisory board members outside of meetings. Share updates, seek further input, and provide progress reports on the implementation of recommendations. This ongoing engagement strengthens the relationship and enhances the value that advisory board members bring to the business.

*"Creating a productive advisory board meeting environment is crucial for harnessing the full potential of your board members' expertise and experience."*

Implementing these best practices for advisory board meetings establishes a strong foundation for effective collaboration, continuous learning, and strategic decision-making. By leveraging the collective wisdom of advisory board members, entrepreneurs can navigate challenges and unlock growth opportunities for their businesses.

|  | Benefits | Implementation |
|---|---|---|
| Establish Clear Meeting Objectives | - Focused discussions<br>- Aligned outcomes | - Communicate objectives in advance<br>- Share meeting agenda |
| Provide Relevant Materials in Advance | - Prepared and informed discussions<br>- In-depth feedback | - Distribute materials beforehand<br>- Allow time for review |
| Foster an Open and Collaborative Environment | - Diverse perspectives<br>- Creative solutions | - Encourage open dialogue<br>- Value every opinion |
| Encourage Active Participation | - Utilize board members' expertise<br>- Broaden insights | - Create an inclusive atmosphere<br>- Invite contributions |
| Allocate Time for Q&A and Discussion | - In-depth insights<br>- Thorough understanding | - Set dedicated discussion time<br>- Encourage questions |
| Take Meeting Minutes | - Reference for future actions<br>- Accountability | - Assign someone to document<br>- Share minutes post-meeting |
| Regular Communication and Follow-Up | - Ongoing engagement<br>- Coordinated efforts | - Maintain communication<br>- Provide progress updates |

## Evaluating the Success of Advisory Boards

When it comes to evaluating the success of advisory boards, it's crucial to measure their impact on key business outcomes. Performance metrics can help gauge the effectiveness of the advisory board and provide valuable insights into its contributions. By tracking metrics such as revenue growth, successful partnerships, or funding secured, businesses can assess the value added by the advisory board and make informed decisions.

Regular assessments should be conducted to ensure that the advisory board remains aligned with the organization's goals. This evaluation process allows businesses to identify areas of improvement and make any necessary adjustments to enhance the board's performance. By continuously evaluating and optimizing the advisory board, businesses can maximize its impact and ensure ongoing success.

*"Regular assessments of an advisory board's performance can reveal opportunities for improvement and alignment with business objectives. By tracking performance metrics, businesses can make data-driven decisions and optimize the contributions of their advisory board."*

## Example Performance Metrics for Evaluating Advisory Boards:

| Metric | Description |
|---|---|
| Revenue Growth | Measure the impact of the advisory board on overall business growth and financial success. |
| Successful Partnerships | Evaluate the advisory board's role in fostering strategic partnerships and collaborations that drive business expansion. |
| Funding Secured | Assess the effectiveness of the advisory board in attracting investment and securing crucial funding for the business. |

By considering these performance metrics and conducting regular assessments, businesses can gain valuable insights into the success and impact of their advisory boards. These evaluations offer the opportunity to optimize the advisory board's contributions, ensure alignment with business goals, and drive continuous improvement.

## Challenges and Pitfalls of Advisory Boards

While advisory boards bring numerous benefits, there are also challenges and potential pitfalls to be aware of. It's important for entrepreneurs to understand and manage these challenges effectively to maximize the value of their advisory board.

## Lack of Engagement from Board Members

One challenge that can arise is a lack of engagement from advisory board members. Board members may have busy schedules or competing priorities, making it difficult for them to dedicate sufficient time and energy to the advisory board. This can lead to ineffective meetings and a diminished impact on the business. To overcome this challenge, entrepreneurs can clearly communicate expectations and establish a culture of commitment and accountability.

## Conflicts of Interest

Conflicts of interest can also pose a challenge when it comes to advisory boards. Board members may have personal or financial interests that could potentially cloud their judgment or impact their ability to provide unbiased advice. Entrepreneurs should carefully select board members who have a track record of integrity and transparency to minimize the risk of conflicts of interest.

## Mismatch Between Business Needs and Advisor Expertise

Another potential pitfall is a mismatch between the needs of the business and the expertise of the advisors. It's essential for entrepreneurs to carefully assess the skills and experience of potential advisory board members and ensure they align with the specific challenges and goals of the business. Regular evaluation and feedback can help identify and address any gaps in expertise.

*"Advisory boards bring diverse perspectives and expertise, but it's crucial for entrepreneurs to actively manage challenges and mitigate potential pitfalls in order to maximize the value they bring to the business."*

| Challenge | Potential Pitfall | Effective Management |
|---|---|---|
| Lack of Engagement | Ineffective meetings and diminished impact on the business | Clear communication of expectations and fostering a culture of commitment and accountability |
| Conflicts of Interest | Potential bias or compromised advice | Selection of board members with a track record of integrity and transparency |
| Mismatch Between Needs and Expertise | Inability to address specific challenges or provide relevant advice | Thorough assessment of advisory board members' skills and ongoing evaluation to address expertise gaps |

Advisory boards are an invaluable asset for businesses, playing a crucial role in shaping strategy, driving growth, and securing funding. By assembling a diverse and effective advisory board, entrepreneurs can tap into a wealth of knowledge, expertise, and insights to propel their businesses forward. These advisory board members provide valuable guidance, helping entrepreneurs make informed decisions and navigate the challenges of running a business.

Implementing best practices when working with advisory boards is essential to maximize their impact. By fostering open communication, setting clear objectives, and providing relevant materials in advance, entrepreneurs can ensure productive advisory board meetings. Regular assessment of the advisory board's performance and alignment with business goals is also crucial to make any necessary adjustments and continuously improve the board's effectiveness. Overall, advisory boards are an integral part of successful businesses, offering valuable support, connections, and strategic guidance. Through their expertise, entrepreneurs can gain new perspectives, access new networks, and make informed decisions. By leveraging the power of advisory boards and actively engaging with them, businesses can position themselves for long-term success.

# Chapter 13

# The Importance of Traction
## Introduction to Traction

In the dynamic world of business, especially startups and ventures in emerging industries, one term that keeps surfacing is 'traction'. But what does it mean? And why does it carry such weight?

Traction is a measure of your business' growth and momentum. It's a demonstration of market demand for your product or service. In essence, traction refers to the progress of a startup company and the momentum it gains as the business grows. To put it simply, it is an indicator that your product or service is solving a problem and that people are willing to pay for your solution.

The importance of traction cannot be overstated. It's not just about having an innovative product or a stellar team. Without traction, even businesses with great potential risk becoming another statistic in the startup graveyard.

There are certain industries where traction plays a particularly vital role. For instance, in the technology sector, which is known for its fast-paced innovation and fierce competition, proving traction can make or break a startup. No matter if you are developing a groundbreaking app or an AI-driven software solution, demonstrating solid traction is crucial.

Investor traction and startup traction are two sides of the same coin. As an entrepreneur, when you are at the helm of a startup, gaining startup traction means getting significant users, customers, pilot customers, or partnerships that validate your business model. And investors value this proof of concept. They do not just invest their money in ideas - they invest in proven concepts backed by traction.

If you are looking to attract investment, ensuring your business has sufficient traction before approaching investors is a smart strategy. Hence the concept of investor traction. The more proven your business concept, the more likely you are to receive funding.

The art of aligning your traction with investor expectations can be tricky but is very rewarding. It involves showcasing your business' traction in a way that matches what investors are looking for - be it growing user numbers, robust revenue growth or expansion into new markets.

### Defining Traction

Moving beyond the general understanding of traction in business, it is important to dive deeper into what exactly constitutes traction. It's not only about increasing sales or reaching more customers, although these factors contribute substantially to gaining traction.

In simple terms, traction can be defined as a quantifiable evidence of market demand for your product or service. The specific metrics used to measure this may vary across industries and based on the individual business model, however some common ones include number of users or customers, rate of user acquisition, and recurring revenue. It underscores an entrepreneur's ability to turn their vision into a viable commercial venture.

At its core, traction involves demonstrating that your business idea isn't just an abstract concept but a reality that is actively solving problems and generating value for your target audience. By doing so, you not only validate your business model but also establish a foundation upon which you could build investor confidence.

### Traction Examples and Case Studies

To understand the concept better, let's consider some real-world examples. A classic example of traction in action is the ride-hailing app Uber. During its early days, Uber showcased significant month-on-month growth in the number of rides booked through its platform. This consistent expansion of its user base was clear evidence of demand for their service which helped them secure successive funding rounds and expand globally.

In another case, Dropbox demonstrated considerable traction by acquiring over 100K email registrations within a single day when they released their explainer video showcasing the unique features and benefits of their product - before they even launched their product!

This kind of traction doesn't happen overnight. It's nurtured over time with calculated strategies, constant testing and tweaks and a solid understanding of your target market, thereby affirming the importance of traction.

But remember, while these are grand examples, traction could be as humble yet impactful as acquiring your first set of loyal customers who found real value in your product and can vouch for it. This can be particularly helpful in the case of startups looking to attract initial investments or bootstrap their operations to achieve growth.

In essence, traction is an undeniable indication that there's something "sticky" about your business —something that resonates with customers and keeps them coming back for more.

## Measuring Traction

After grasping what traction entails and seeing how it can play out in real-world businesses, the next step is understanding how we measure this elusive concept. How do you tell if your startup is gaining traction? What measurable figures do you look at to ensure your business is on the right path?

Traction metrics, also known as Key Performance Indicators (KPIs), are generally used to assess the success or progress of a business. These metrics vary from industry to industry and even between different types of businesses in the same industry. As such, it's crucial for every entrepreneur to identify which metrics are most appropriate for their venture.

Some common metrics include the number of active users, customer acquisition costs, lifetime value of a customer, churn rate (the percentage of customers who stop using your product over a certain period), and conversion rates. But remember, what matters most is not just the numbers themselves but their growth over time.

## The Role of Traction Metrics in Business Growth

Understanding traction metrics helps startups determine if they're moving in the right direction. If a business model isn't working as expected, these indicators will show that something's amiss early enough for entrepreneurs to make necessary adjustments. By doing so, you mitigate risks and increase your odds of success significantly.

Moreover, tracking these metrics can provide valuable insights into which aspects of your business are working well and which areas need improvement. For instance, if your user acquisition cost is too high while your average revenue per user is low, then scaling up might only lead to bigger losses. However, with this information at hand, you can tweak your strategies to optimize profits before embarking on expansive growth initiatives.

## The Importance of Competitive Benchmarking

In addition, measuring traction isn't just restricted to analyzing your venture's internal data. It also involves looking at competitor research and industry benchmarks. This competitive benchmarking provides valuable context for measuring traction.

For instance, having a churn rate of 2% might seem impressive on its own. But if the industry average is 1%, then your business might be underperforming compared to peers. Thus, understanding how your venture stacks up against others in the industry can provide a more accurate picture of your progress.

## Caution in Choosing and Using Metrics

While metrics are undeniably essential in measuring traction, entrepreneurs should however exercise caution in choosing and interpreting these numbers. Not all metrics are equally important for every business, and focusing on the wrong ones could lead to misguided strategies.

The best approach is often to focus on a few key metrics that are most relevant for your specific business model, rather than trying to monitor everything simultaneously. Also, instead of merely chasing impressive figures, it's crucial to understand what each metric implies about your business performance and make informed decisions based on that understanding.

In conclusion, measuring traction is an integral part of any startup's journey - providing insight into its growth trajectory and offering valuable cues for strategic decision making.

## Building and Strategizing Traction

The journey to success for any business, particularly startups, is dotted with numerous challenges. Among the myriad factors that determinetheir survival is their aptitude in building and strategizing on traction from its nascent stages. This involves meticulous planning and calculated risk-taking.

A key facet of building traction is continuous product development. It begins with identifying a genuine market need and then creating a solution for it that can be monetized. But innovation doesn't stop there. Businesses should constantly refine their offerings based on customer feedback and changes in market trends to maintain or grow their user base.

Further, strategic marketing plays an instrumental role in traction building efforts. Crafting unique selling propositions, targeting the right audience segments, nurturing leads and optimizing conversion rates - all are critical elements in driving awareness about your products or services and influencing buying decisions. The priority should be to build brand equity among prospective customers which can propel organic growth through word-of-mouth referrals.

## Traction through Fundraising

Fundraising too can significantly boost your startup's traction. By securing investment from venture capitalists or angel investors, not only does it provide necessary capital infusion for growth, but it also increases credibility among stakeholders - making your startup attractive for future rounds of financing.

However, attracting investors isn't easy; it calls for a compelling narrative about your business' potential backed by credible evidence of progress - essentially showcasing your traction in fundraising. This includes demonstrating steady revenue growth, increasing user acquisition rates or even qualitative achievements like key partnerships or patents won.

## Traction Strategies: An Entrepreneurial Pathway

Entrepreneurship often accelerates the path to gaining traction. By interacting directly with the market – be it customers, competitors or potential investors – entrepreneurs can gather invaluable feedback and insights. This can lead to pivot moments, opening avenues for new business models or revenue streams thereby helping in building traction.

Moreover, entrepreneurship also involves creating a culture of innovation and resilience within an organisation which is essential for achieving sustainable growth. Whether it's about fostering teamwork, encouraging creative problem-solving or cultivating commitment to deliver value to customers – these soft aspects of the business often fuel hard metrics like user growth and revenue.

## A Look at Traction Strategies from Competitor Research

Another vital strategy to build traction is learning from what's working for others - essentially doing competitor research. While blindly copying competitors may not succeed given unique market positioning and customer preferences, certain trends or practices could be adapted or improved upon.

For instance, if competitor books suggest that investments in automation technologies are leading to significant productivity gains and customer satisfaction, businesses could consider implementing this in their operations. Similarly, understanding how your rivals are leveraging digital marketing tactics could offer fresh perspectives on improving your own online presence.

In essence, building traction requires strategic planning and execution; a blend of internal innovation as well as adapting proven industry practices. But remember that gaining traction isn't a quick win play; it's a long-term game requiring perseverance, adaptability and above all else - an unwavering focus on delivering value.

## Showcasing Traction to Investors

Getting traction is one thing, but the ability to effectively showcase it to potential investors is another crucial aspect that startups should master. Raising funds for your venture largely boils down to convincing investors that your business has significant growth potential and they would gain a good return on their investment. Demonstrating solid traction can be instrumental in this process.

When meeting with prospective investors, you're essentially selling the story of your startup - its past progress, present status, and future prospects. Instead of just sharing impressive numbers or flamboyant features, focus on conveying the real value your product or service delivers. Use facts and figures as supporting elements to substantiate your story.

This could include indicators such as an increasing user or customer base proving growing market demand, consistent revenue generation validating commercial viability, or strategic partnerships emphasizing collaborative growth opportunities. Remember that each metric you share should ideally communicate something significant about your business' value proposition and why it stands out in the market.

## Leveraging Examples to Showcase Traction

Narratives are powerful persuaders in human communications. Consider using examples from your business's journey so far to highlight key instances of showcasing traction. Perhaps there was a pivotal moment when you significantly increased user acquisition or a unique marketing initiative that drove substantial engagement. Share these stories – they add depth and credibility to your pitch.

Note that even early-stage startups with limited operational history can still demonstrate traction by showcasing qualitative achievements such as securing patent rights for a unique technology, gaining recognition in industry events or launching MVPs (Minimum Viable Products) successfully.

## Making Powerful First Impressions

Your initial interaction with potential investors sets the tone for all subsequent communication. Hence, focusing on making a convincing first impression can go a long way in securing their interest and confidence.

This isn't merely about dressing up your number sheets or sprucing up your product demos – it involves presenting a persuasive case for why your venture is worth betting on. Also take into account the specific interests of the investors you're approaching. For instance, if an investor has a keen interest in sustainable business models, be sure to emphasize how your startup aligns with such concerns.

## Drawing Inspiration from Competitor Success Stories

A smart strategy while showcasing traction can involve studying competitor success stories to derive valuable insights. This doesn't mean simply mimicking their approach, but understanding what worked for them and adapting those elements in a way that aligns with your unique business context.

Remember that building trust and excitement among investors doesn't have to rely solely on standalone metrics; it should ideally paint a comprehensive picture of your venture's journey - past, present and future - underscoring how you've overcome challenges, leveraged opportunities and are well-positioned for success ahead.

# Chapter 14

# Building a Robust Business Model

The onset of the digital era, characterized by rapidly evolving technological advancements and shifts in consumer behavior, has compelled businesses worldwide to rethink their conventional business models. In this transforming landscape, merely having a standard set of operations or steadfast strategy is not enough. It's now crucial for firms to continuously reinvent their approaches to stay relevant, productive, and profitable.

As we traverse through this narrative, we will explore the components that constitute a robust business model, including varied revenue streams and cost structures. Additionally, we will see how organizations can pivot their operations without sacrificing investor confidence. We aim to bring you an insightful guide on creating a robust and adaptable business model that can thrive amidst the ever-changing global business environment.

When assessing any potent business model's crux, it involves understanding its foundations – the essential elements that contribute to its strength and longevity. Be it technological giants like Airbnb or start-ups carving out their niche in competitive markets, every durable business model comprises certain common components.

Having a clearly defined value proposition at the forefront allows companies to distinguish themselves from competitors. Airbnb is an excellent example of this aspect – they didn't just change the way people stay away from home; they transformed the travel and hospitality industry by bringing 'living like a local' to the masses.

Furthermore, companies need a comprehensive understanding of their target audience, knowing precisely who their products/services are for. This insight informs every facet of a company's operations from product development to marketing strategies.

The importance of efficient channels can't be overstated. These are means by which the company delivers its value proposition to its customers. Recognizing appropriate channels – both paths to customers and routes for revenue flow – hinges upon a deep understanding of customer behaviors and preferences.

Lastly, it is vital to have strong customer relationships. The ability to anticipate and respond to customer needs effectively determines how resilient your business model is amidst market shifts.

Such robust business models don't just materialize overnight but are a product of iterative learning, strategic planning, and conscious implementation. They are grounded by solid components while remaining flexible enough to pivot as per evolving market dynamics.

As we move further into the digital age, businesses can no longer afford to be static and uninspiring in their operational approach. The broader business landscape is continuously evolving, with new technologies disrupting traditional industries, shifts in economic conditions, and unprecedented global events causing ripple effects across sectors. Let's look at these factors that warrant iterative development in business models.

For instance, the technology, media, and telecommunications industry witnessed significant global M&A trends, leading to an increased demand for innovative solutions and services. Businesses operating within this space need a dynamic model that allows them to capitalize on these mergers and acquisitions effectively. Alternatively, governmental bodies worldwide are undergoing changes in their military's defense budget overview, which directly impacts defense contractors and suppliers. To navigate such volatile situations, businesses should have a model that accommodates swift adaptations while minimizing disruption to operations.

Moreover, understanding the world economic outlook is crucial for any organization looking to thrive in an unpredictable global market. Recent events like Brexit or trade wars can impact various sectors differently, making it imperative for businesses to stay informed about macroeconomic trends. This information aids companies in predicting potential risks and adjusting strategies accordingly, thus maintaining their agility in the face of adversity.

The world has undeniably gone through a phase shift due to the COVID-19 pandemic, with subsequent repercussions expected over the coming years. Some industries prospered amidst this chaos while others fell. Therefore, analyzing the global risks report regularly can help organizations identify potential threats or opportunities early on, enabling them to recalibrate their business model swiftly.

To stay relevant amidst such dynamic circumstances would require continuous innovation driven by a profound understanding of these changes.

A case in point is Airbnb's evolution over time—this successful platform smartly adapted to changing market needs, redefining its value proposition, and restructuring its operations accordingly. Their model now caters to a wide range of customer needs - from affordable accommodation for travelers to unique experiences for locals and tourists alike.

Another instance is how banks had to adjust their operating models in response to the evolution of Fintech. As customers demanded more functionality and convenience, traditional brick-and-mortar banks had to incorporate digital services into their model to stay competitive.

Collectively, these instances stress the need for businesses to cultivate an adaptable mindset when building their models—one capable of embracing change, whether it's significant shifts in global trends or nuanced alterations within their industry.

**Financial Underpinnings**

As we have established, businesses need to be dynamic and adaptable in order to succeed in our rapidly changing global landscape. This includes understanding the financial underpinnings of their models and being able to adjust these as necessary. In this part of our guide, we will delve into the crucial aspects of revenue generation and cost structures.

Revenue streams are the bread and butter of any business model. Whether it's from sales of products or services, licensing, subscription fees, or advertising, companies must identify where their income is coming from. A robust business model should have diverse revenue streams that ensure stable income even when market conditions change.

For instance, a major shift seen with the rise of digital platforms has been an increased reliance on subscription-based models. Companies like Netflix and Spotify, previously unheard-of entities in traditional media industries, understood early on that they could generate consistent revenue through monthly subscriptions for their streaming services instead of one-off purchases. These examples illustrate how innovative companies can leverage technological advancements and evolving consumer preferences to create new sources of revenue.

Another important topic regarding revenue is the capability of generating sufficient profits to meet operating expenses, which brings us to another critical feature: cost structures. Every business incurs costs - ranging from raw materials purchasing and labor costs to administrative expenses and marketing budgets. By identifying all its costs and consistently monitoring them, a company can develop strategies for reducing unnecessary expenses while investing efficiently in growth-driving activities.

The choice of cost structure largely depends on the sector within which the company operates. For example, startup companies often have higher operating costs due to initial investments in technology or talent. However, as they scale up and realize economies of scale, these costs typically decrease.

In contrast, large corporations might employ different online marketing strategies for increasing sales revenues. This may involve investing heavily in digital advertising or social media marketing, with the aim of reaching a wider audience and driving more sales. Thus, they might have higher marketing expenses but also reap greater profits due to increased sales.

The key takeaway here is that companies should regularly review their revenue generation strategies and cost structures. It's not enough to build them once and forget about them. Businesses must be proactive in adjusting them to current market realities, customer behaviors, and technological advancements.

Therefore, revenue streams and cost structures aren't static components of your business model; they are dynamic elements that you need to actively manage. Having a clear understanding of these economic fundamentals can equip any organization with the tools necessary to maintain financial health while facing ever-changing market situations.

## Agility and Adaptibillity

While having a robust business model with dynamic revenue streams and sound cost structures is significant, another key factor that can make or break a company's survival in today's fast-paced market is its agility and adaptability. Institutional resilience isn't about bracing for disaster—it's about creating an organization that is capable of responding quickly to change without losing investor confidence. So, let's delve into how organizations can embrace agile and customer-centric cultures; fundamental ingredients in constructing resilient business models.

Firstly, adopting an agile approach to business operations isn't just limited to technology or software development firms; it has now become a necessity across all industries. An agile business model means being able to respond faster and more effectively to changes; it involves iterating on products based on user feedback, adapting services according to market trends, or changing strategic directions at short notice if necessary.

This flexibility not only ensures that businesses can maneuver through unexpected situations but also helps them stay ahead of competitors in a rapidly evolving marketplace. Furthermore, the ability to iterate quickly allows companies to test out new ideas and innovations without the risk of large-scale failure—thereby fostering an environment conducive for innovation and growth.

The story of Nokia's downfall serves as an excellent lesson here. Once a global leader in mobile phones, Nokia was too slow to react when smartphones entered the scene. Their inflexible business model combined with reluctance towards innovation led to their eventual downfall.

Apart from agility, maintaining investor confidence requires businesses to adopt a customer-centric culture. Understanding customer needs and preferences should form the cornerstone of any business model. When companies place the customer at the center of their decisions—from product development to sales—they are more likely to build loyal customer bases that contribute significantly to long-term profitability.

Moreover, a customer-oriented approach can also increase investor confidence. After all, satisfied customers equate to higher revenues and better business growth prospects—factors that are bound to attract investors.

However, while pivoting might be necessary for survival, it's equally crucial to ensure a smooth transition that doesn't affect investor confidence negatively. Investors typically prefer stability and dichotomous changes may raise concerns about future profitability. Therefore, when implementing significant changes to the business model, clear communication regarding these shifts and their necessity is essential.

The exemplar of Adobe Systems showcases how pivoting the business model effectively can reap impressive rewards. When they shifted from selling packaged software to a subscription-based cloud service, they ensured seamless communication with their investors regarding the overall strategy and expected benefits. Consequently, despite initial bumps post-transition, Adobe managed its pivot successfully without losing investor confidence—resulting in higher recurring revenues today.

In conclusion, businesses seeking to create durable models must strive for agility by embracing change, maintaining a customer-centric approach, and ensuring transparent communication when maneuvering through significant strategic shifts. By adhering to these strategies, companies can not only secure their survival but also elevate their standing in today's dynamic marketplace.

## Summation & Looking Ahead

In today's rapidly transforming business landscape, reinvention is more than just a buzzword. It has become an essential trait of businesses aiming to stay competitive, relevant, and profitable in the long run. Hence, businesses need to adopt robust models that can weather adversities while capitalizing on opportunities.

Reinventing your business model does not necessarily mean a complete overhaul of your existing operations. But it does imply adapting to the changing market dynamics, innovating your products or services, and revamping your strategies to outperform competitors. For instance, think about how Amazon went from being an online bookstore to a one-stop shop for almost everything under the sun. This was only possible due to its willingness to evolve with consumer preferences and technological advancements.

The concept of reinvention also involves shunning obsolete practices that no longer serve you well. In doing so, organisations can make room for fresh ideas and innovative practices that will propel them forward.

A key example of a successful business model reinvention is Netflix's transition from a DVD rental service to an online streaming giant. They recognized early on the market potential for streaming content and made necessary changes to their business model accordingly. This pivot was instrumental in their tremendous success today.

In this age of digital disruption, the sector that perhaps stands most at the precipice of change is jobs and job training. The surge towards automation, AI, and remote work structures necessitates a relook into traditional hiring and training manners. Companies need to adapt to these shifts by envisaging the *'Future of jobs and job training'*, creating agile workflows and learning solutions which prepare employees for this new world order.

But remember, reinventing your business does not guarantee immediate results or profits; it's a journey filled with trial and error, unpredictability, and continuous learning. It's about creating a culture where setbacks are stepping stones to improvement and where critical thinking forms the basis of decision-making.

As we navigate this digital wave, standing still is moving backward. We must continue challenging norms, pushing boundaries, and transforming our ways. This constant reinvention—understanding changing customer needs, addressing global trends, and leveraging technological evolution—is not just recommended; it's a necessity for survival and success in today's business world.

To put it succinctly, "Change is the only constant". So let us embrace this paradigm shift, create resilient business models that can weather storms and seize opportunities alike, all while continuing to deliver value to our customers. Let's forge ahead into an era marked by innovation and agility, with our eyes fixed on progress and growth.

# Chapter 15

# Risk Mitigation Strategies

Risk mitigation strategies are crucial for protecting your business plan against potential setbacks and ensuring investor confidence. By identifying potential risks in your business plan and developing strategies to mitigate them, you can minimize the negative impact of unforeseen events and enhance the chances of success for your venture.

**Key Takeaways:**

- Implementing risk mitigation strategies is essential for ensuring investor confidence in your business plan.
- Identify potential risks in your business plan and develop strategies to mitigate them.
- Minimize the negative impact of unforeseen events by being prepared with risk mitigation strategies.
- Risk mitigation strategies increase the chances of success for your venture.
- Investors are more likely to be confident in your business plan if they see that you have considered and addressed potential setbacks.

**Understanding Risk Management**

Risk management is a crucial aspect of protecting your business from potential threats and minimizing the consequences of unforeseen events. By creating effective risk management strategies, you can mitigate vulnerabilities and ensure the long-term success of your venture.

One of the first steps in risk management is understanding the threats that your business may face. These threats can be categorized into different types such as environmental, manmade, internal, and external. By identifying these threats, you can assess the risks associated with each and develop appropriate mitigation measures.

*"Risk management involves creating a level of protection that mitigates vulnerabilities to threats and reduces potential consequences."*

A thorough threat assessment is essential in determining the value of your assets and cataloging the potential risks. This assessment helps you prioritize your risk management efforts and allocate resources effectively.

By proactively identifying and managing vulnerabilities, you can minimize the impact of potential risks and protect your business from various consequences, including financial loss, reputation damage, and operational disruption.

**Risk Assessment and Testing**

Risk assessment plays a vital role in ensuring the security and stability of your technology assets. By conducting thorough testing and vulnerability assessments, you can identify and mitigate potential risks, safeguarding your business from potential threats.

Different testing techniques are used to assess vulnerabilities and evaluate the effectiveness of security measures. These include:

1. *Automated vulnerability scans:* These scans use specialized software to detect common vulnerabilities in your systems, such as outdated software versions or configuration errors.
2. *Intrusive vulnerability scans:* These scans go beyond automated tools and simulate real-world hacking attempts to uncover more complex vulnerabilities and weaknesses.
3. *Penetration tests:* Also known as pen tests, these tests involve authorized "ethical hacking" attempts to exploit your systems' vulnerabilities. Penetration tests provide valuable insights into potential weaknesses and help validate security controls.

It's crucial to obtain proper authorization for conducting penetration tests to ensure legal compliance and minimize any potential retaliation from automated security systems or third parties.

Ultimately, risk assessment and testing help you proactively identify and address vulnerabilities, allowing you to strengthen your security measures and protect your business from potential threats.

*"Risk assessment and testing are essential for protecting your technology assets and ensuring the stability of your systems. By proactively evaluating vulnerabilities and addressing them, you can fortify your defenses against potential threats."*

**Example: Vulnerabilities Detection**

| Vulnerability | Description | Risk Level |
|---|---|---|
| Outdated Software | Running software versions with known security vulnerabilities. | High |
| Weak Passwords | Using easily guessable or common passwords. | Medium |
| Unpatched Systems | Failing to apply necessary security updates and patches. | High |
| Insufficient Access Controls | Granting unauthorized individuals access to sensitive data or systems. | Medium |

This example highlights some of the common vulnerabilities that can be detected through risk assessment and testing. By prioritizing and addressing these vulnerabilities, businesses can significantly reduce their exposure to potential threats.

**Change Management**

Change management is a crucial methodology for making modifications to information systems while keeping track of changes. It plays a vital role in ensuring the smooth functioning of organizations by managing the impact of changes and minimizing any associated risks. An effective change management process involves documentation and the formation of a dedicated change management team consisting of representatives from IT, network security, and upper management.

*"Change management is all about ensuring that changes are implemented smoothly, minimizing disruptions and maximizing the benefits."*

A key aspect of change management is the documentation of changes. This involves capturing details about the system architecture, file or document classification, and any modifications made to them. By maintaining proper documentation, organizations can easily track the changes, identify potential risks, and ensure compliance with industry standards and regulations.

**Risk and Impact Assessment**

One of the primary responsibilities of the change management team is to review proposed changes and assess their potential risks and impact. This involves conducting a thorough evaluation to determine any potential negative consequences that may arise from implementing the change. By assessing risks and impacts in advance, organizations can proactively plan mitigation strategies, allocate resources effectively, and minimize the chance of any adverse effects on business operations.

*"The change management team plays a pivotal role in ensuring that changes are implemented in a manner that aligns with the organization's goals and minimizes disruptions."*

The change management team acts as a bridge between the technical teams and upper management by thoroughly evaluating the proposed changes and providing recommendations. Their expertise and knowledge enable them to consider various factors, such as technical feasibility, potential risks, resource requirements, and impact on various stakeholders. This collaborative approach ensures that changes are implemented in a controlled and well-planned manner.

Change management is an essential component of effective risk mitigation and maintaining the stability of information systems. By documenting changes and involving a dedicated change management team, organizations can ensure the smooth transition of modifications, minimize disruptions, and safeguard the overall integrity and security of their systems.

## Privilege Management

Privilege management plays a vital role in maintaining the security and integrity of your organization's data. By effectively assigning and revoking access privileges, you can ensure that only authorized individuals have the necessary level of access to sensitive information. This helps prevent unauthorized access and reduces the risk of data breaches.

Access levels are a fundamental aspect of privilege management. They determine the extent of access that an individual or user group has to specific resources, such as files or systems. By defining access levels based on job roles and responsibilities, you can ensure that employees have the appropriate level of access needed to perform their duties, while minimizing the risk of unauthorized access.

Privilege auditing is an essential part of privilege management. It involves regularly reviewing the access privileges assigned to individuals or user groups to ensure that they align with current job roles and responsibilities. This auditing process helps identify any inconsistencies or unauthorized privileges, allowing for corrective action to be taken promptly. By conducting privilege audits, organizations can proactively address any potential risks and maintain a strong security posture.

## Key Benefits of Privilege Management:

*"Privilege management helps organizations prevent unauthorized access, maintain data security, and adhere to regulatory requirements. By effectively managing access privileges, organizations can reduce the risk of data breaches and ensure that employees only have access to the resources they need."*

Implementing a comprehensive privilege management strategy is crucial for protecting your organization's sensitive information and maintaining data security. By assigning access levels based on job roles and conducting regular privilege audits, you can minimize the risk of unauthorized access and prevent security breaches.

| Benefits of Privilege Management | Description |
|---|---|
| Data Security | Privilege management ensures that only authorized individuals have access to sensitive information, reducing the risk of data breaches. |
| Regulatory Compliance | By managing access privileges and conducting regular audits, organizations can demonstrate compliance with regulatory requirements. |
| Risk Mitigation | Effective privilege management helps identify and address potential risks, minimizing the likelihood of unauthorized access and data breaches. |

## Incident Management

Effective incident management plays a critical role in safeguarding businesses and minimizing the impact of unexpected events. It involves a structured approach to identify, analyze, contain, and resolve incidents, ensuring a swift return to normal operations with minimal disruption.

One key aspect of incident management is incident response, which focuses on promptly identifying, analyzing, and containing incidents as they occur. This allows organizations to mitigate the immediate impact of the incident and prevent it from escalating further.

Incident handling is another crucial component of incident management, involving the planning, coordination, and communication necessary to resolve incidents effectively. By establishing clear protocols and workflows, organizations can streamline their response efforts and ensure efficient collaboration among relevant stakeholders.

## Fire Protection Systems in Incident Management

Fire protection systems play a vital role in incident management, especially in dealing with fire-related incidents. These systems are designed to detect, control, and suppress fires, protecting lives, assets, and operations.

Fire detection systems, such as smoke detectors and heat sensors, play a crucial role in identifying potential fire incidents early on. These systems can provide timely alerts, allowing for a swift response to prevent the spread of fire and minimize damage.

Fire suppression systems, including sprinklers and fire extinguishers, are essential components of incident management, as they help to control and extinguish fires. These systems are strategically installed to suppress the fire promptly and reduce its impact on the affected area.

Proper installation, regular maintenance, and routine testing of fire protection systems are critical to ensure their reliability and effectiveness. Organizations should adhere to relevant fire safety codes and regulations, as well as engage qualified professionals to design, install, and inspect these systems.

## Incident Management Process

Below is an overview of the incident management process, highlighting the key steps involved:

| Step | Description |
|---|---|
| 1. Identification | Identifying and recognizing an incident or potential incident. |
| 2. Analysis | Evaluating the incident's severity, impact, and potential risks. |
| 3. Containment | Taking immediate actions to contain the incident and prevent further damage. |
| 4. Resolution | Implementing measures to resolve the incident and restore normal operations. |
| 5. Post-Incident Review | Conducting a thorough review to analyze the incident's cause and identify areas for improvement. |
| 6. Documentation | Documenting all relevant details of the incident, including actions taken and lessons learned. |

By following a structured incident management process, organizations can effectively address incidents, minimize their impact, and improve overall resilience in the face of unforeseen events.

## Risk Calculation

Assessing the likelihood and impact of risks is a crucial step in effective risk management. Risk calculation provides valuable insights into the potential consequences of a risk event and helps prioritize mitigation efforts. There are two main approaches to risk calculation: qualitative and quantitative risk calculation.

## Qualitative Risk Calculation

In qualitative risk calculation, observation and expert judgment are used to assess and assign numeric values or labels to represent the level of risk. This approach is based on subjective assessment and allows for a qualitative understanding of the risks involved. Qualitative risk calculation provides a broad overview of risks and helps in identifying potential areas of concern.

## Quantitative Risk Calculation

Quantitative risk calculation, on the other hand, relies on historical data and statistical analysis to calculate the likelihood and impact of a risk event. This approach uses quantifiable data and mathematical models to generate "hard" numbers associated with the probability and severity of risks. Quantitative risk calculation provides a more precise and objective assessment of risks, enabling informed decision-making.

Tools such as Mean Time Between Failure (MTBF) and Annualized Rate of Occurrence (ARO) are commonly used in quantitative risk calculation. MTBF helps predict the average time between failures for a system or equipment, while ARO estimates the rate at which a specific risk event may occur in a given period.

*"Quantitative risk calculation allows us to make data-driven decisions and prioritize our risk mitigation efforts based on the level of impact and probability. It helps us allocate resources effectively and minimize potential losses."*

| Risk Category | Likelihood | Impact |
|---|---|---|
| Natural Disasters | Low | High |
| Security Breach | Medium | High |
| Financial Risks | High | Medium |
| Operational Risks | Medium | Medium |
| Regulatory Compliance | Low | Low |

**Implementing Risk Mitigation Programs**

Implementing risk mitigation programs is a critical step in safeguarding your business against potential setbacks. By carefully planning and executing these programs, you can minimize the impact of risks and ensure the continuity of your operations. There are two types of impairments to consider: preplanned impairments and emergency impairments.

**Preplanned Impairments**

Preplanned impairments are authorized actions that are taken proactively to address potential interruptions or failures. These impairments are carefully planned and executed to minimize risks and ensure the safety and reliability of your business operations. The authorization for preplanned impairments is granted by the impairment coordinator, who oversees the process and ensures that all necessary controls are in place.

**Emergency Impairments**

Emergency impairments, on the other hand, involve immediate actions taken in response to unexpected interruptions or failures. When a critical risk arises, it is essential to address it promptly to prevent further damage and mitigate the impact on your business. Immediate notification should be made to relevant parties, such as the fire department and insurance carrier, to ensure proper assistance and support.

Implementing risk mitigation programs also involves conducting regular inspections and risk assessments to identify potential vulnerabilities. Based on these assessments, recommendations can be made to mitigate risks and enhance the overall security and resilience of your business. This can include implementing necessary controls, such as fire watches or temporary water supplies, to address specific risks.

By incorporating risk mitigation programs into your business strategy, you can proactively protect your operations and assets from potential setbacks. Whether through preplanned impairments or emergency actions, these programs provide a framework for managing risks and ensuring the continuity of your business.

**Integrating Risk Management into Operations**

Risk management plays a vital role in the success of any organization. To ensure the seamless execution of operations, it is crucial to integrate risk management into the planning and execution phases. By proactively assessing and managing risks, businesses can anticipate potential difficulties and determine the most effective course of action.

Resource allocation is a key consideration when making risk decisions. Balancing the benefits and costs of each option helps in optimizing resource allocation and maximizing the overall effectiveness of risk management strategies.

When integrating risk management into operations, it is important to consider the following:

1. **Planning Phase:** Incorporate risk management practices from the beginning of the planning phase. Identify potential risks and evaluate their potential impact on operations. This allows for the development of strategies to mitigate these risks before they occur.

2. **Execution Phase:** Implement risk management measures during the execution of operations. Regularly monitor and assess risks, making necessary adjustments to mitigate them effectively.

3. **Resource Allocation:** Consider resource allocation when making risk-related decisions. Evaluate the costs, benefits, and potential impact of different risk mitigation strategies to allocate resources efficiently.

By integrating risk management into operations, organizations can significantly enhance their ability to navigate uncertainties, minimize disruptions, and ensure the smooth execution of business plans.

*"Integrating risk management into the core functions of an organization is imperative for long-term success and sustainability. It enables businesses to anticipate challenges, allocate resources effectively, and respond proactively to mitigate risks."*

Risk Management Integration Framework

| Phase | Activities |
|-------|-----------|
| Planning | - Identify potential risks<br>- Evaluate impact on operations<br>- Develop strategies to mitigate risks |
| Execution | - Implement risk management measures<br>- Monitor and assess risks<br>- Adjust strategies to mitigate risks |
| Resource Allocation | - Evaluate costs, benefits, and impact<br>- Allocate resources efficiently |

**Key Principles of ORM**

Operational Risk Management (ORM) is essential for organizations to effectively manage risks, optimize gains, and prevent or mitigate losses. ORM is guided by four key principles:

1. Accepting no unnecessary risk: Organizations should identify and eliminate any risks that are deemed unnecessary or pose unnecessary harm. By minimizing unnecessary risks, organizations can safeguard their operations and resources.

2. **Making risk decisions at the appropriate level:** In ORM, risk decisions should be made by individuals who have the necessary expertise and authority. By delegating risk decisions to the appropriate level, organizations can ensure that decisions are well-informed and aligned with the overall objectives.

3. **Accepting risk when benefits outweigh costs:** ORM involves weighing the potential benefits against the costs associated with accepting risks. Organizations should assess the risk-benefit ratio and make informed decisions based on a thorough risk-benefit analysis. This allows for a balanced approach in managing risks and maximizing operational capability.

4. **Integrating ORM into planning at all levels:** Organizations should integrate ORM into their planning processes at all levels of operation. This includes proactive risk assessment, risk mitigation strategies, and resource allocation. By embedding ORM

into planning, organizations can enhance their ability to anticipate and mitigate potential risks, while optimizing resource allocation for better risk management. By adhering to these key principles of ORM, organizations can enhance their risk management practices, minimize unnecessary risk, and make informed risk decisions based on a comprehensive risk-benefit analysis. This ultimately contributes to the overall success and resilience of the organization.

Chapter 16

# Market Analysis and Fit
**Introduction and Importance of Market Analysis for Start-ups**

In today's highly competitive business environment, comprehension of the market that your start-up intends to penetrate is pivotal. At the heart of every successful business venture lies thorough, strategic and conscientious market analysis. It involves a detailed examination of elements in your industry, including market segmentation, defining target market, and crafting marketing strategies — facets that eventually shape up your company's future trajectory.

Market analysis essentially equips you with insights into current market conditions, helping you understand where your customers exist, what attracts them, and how you can cater to their needs effectively. But its importance doesn't stop at customer understanding. Known for their dynamic nature, markets constantly evolve. A sound market analysis helps start-ups anticipate changes, identify opportunities, and react swiftly to any shifts in market trends before competitors do.

## Market Segmentation
The first step towards conducting an effective market analysis is segmenting your market. Market segmentation involves breaking down your potential customers into distinct groups based on specific attributes like demographics, buying habits, lifestyle etc. The key purpose here is to identify niche segments whose needs align with your product or service offerings.

For instance, if you're introducing an innovative tech-gadget into the market, your primary segment might be tech-savvy millennials with a high inclination towards novel technology products. Identifying such segments helps tailor your marketing efforts to resonate better with these subsets of consumers, enhancing both effectiveness and efficiency of marketing campaigns.

## Defining Target Market
Upon sorting your market into manageable segments, the next step is defining your target market. In simple terms, this is the specific segment (or segments) your product or service is most likely to appeal to. Defining your target market brings precision to your marketing efforts. Rather than adopting a 'one-size-fits-all' approach, focusing on a defined group enables you to formulate targeted strategies, produce tailored messages, and establish deeper connections with your customers.

## Crafting Marketing Strategies
With a clear understanding of your target market, crafting marketing strategies becomes a more feasible task. A good marketing strategy subtly blends both creativity and data-driven insights, ensuring that your business responds proactively to market trends and consumer behavior. It involves choosing the right channels to reach your audience, creating compelling content relevant to them, setting realistic outcomes, and assessing progress periodically to make necessary tweaks. This loops back to the significance of market analysis - it forms the backbone for all such strategic decisions.

To sum it up, conducting a comprehensive market analysis is akin to plotting a roadmap for your start-up's journey. It empowers you with knowledge about who exactly your customers are, where they exist in vast markets, what they need, and how best you can meet those needs. Thus, setting the stage for sustainable growth and success in the long run.

## Detailed Description on Conducting Market Research and Analysis
Having established the need for market analysis, let's delve deeper into the process of conducting successful market research. To start with, market research is not a one-size-fits-all

approach but rather an in-depth study that leverages both quantitative (statistical) and qualitative (observational) data to uncover insights about potential customers, their behavior patterns, preferences, and demographic attributes.

An excellent example of successful market research is Amazon. By conducting rigorous market research coupled with sophisticated AI technologies, Amazon has been able to predict customer behavior with remarkable accuracy. This has allowed them to offer personalized product recommendations, enhancing their user experience and boosting sales.

## Gaining Insights About Potential Customers

The primary objective of conducting market research is to gain deeper insights into who your potential customers are. Initially, this involves gathering data related to their demographics such as age group, gender, income level, occupation etc.

However, it's crucial to remember that potential customers are more than just statistical figures - they're individuals with unique needs and preferences. Therefore, apart from demographic information gathering, understanding psychographic attributes like interests, lifestyles, values and buying behaviors is equally crucial.

## Understanding Customer Preferences

While ensuring your product or service meets a particular need in the market is important, understanding what else drives customer choices can provide you a competitive edge. Do they prefer high-quality products over cheaper alternatives? What features do they prioritize? Understanding these aspects will help shape your product offering and marketing efforts accordingly.

## Customer Demographics

Demographics reveal much about the economic circumstances that influence a consumer's buying power. For instance, higher-income groups might be more willing to splurge on premium products, while millennials might have a stronger preference towards eco-friendly offerings. Catering to these details will ensure your product resonates with the right audience.

## Factors Influencing Customer Decisions

Lastly, understanding the factors influencing customer decisions can provide valuable insights. These factors could be anything from economic conditions, societal trends, personal preferences or even emotional triggers. For example, during a recession, consumers may prioritize price over brand loyalty.

Understanding these decision-making factors not only helps you craft a relevant marketing strategy but also predict future consumer behavior and market movement. Thus, effective market research aids in planning for contingencies and ensuring sustainable business growth despite market uncertainties.

To conclude, conducting successful market research involves much more than gathering raw statistics—it's a detailed study that combines both hard data and behavioral analysis to understand potential customers better.

## Focus on User Personas

Defining user personas or marketing personas is a critical aspect of market analysis and business growth. It refers to the process of outlining fictitious characters based on your range of potential or existing customers. These personas typically encompass key aspects such as demographics, behavior patterns, motivations, and goals.

Creating user personas helps businesses tailor their products and services, online presence, communication channels, and everything in between to meet the specific needs and preferences of different customer segments. This personalization strategy enables businesses to understand their audience segments better, making marketing efforts more effective.

## The Process of Defining User Personas

To define user personas effectively, a start-up should begin by conducting in-depth research into its target customer base. Relying on data from past customer interactions, market research, customer feedback and social media can provide valuable insights into who these personas are. Next comes the grouping stage – segmenting similar customers together based on common characteristics to create distinct buckets. The persona defined should be a representative for each group. Remember, it's not about capturing every customer but instead focusing on the primary groups your start-up aims to serve.

## Benefits of Having Well-Defined User Personas

User personas offer myriad advantages when it comes to better understanding your audience segments. They help clarify who exactly you're targeting with your product or service offering, thus guiding the development process by aligning it with specific customer needs and wants.

In terms of marketing approaches too, knowing accurately who you're talking to makes crafting compelling narratives a lot easier. This aids more engaging content creation targeted at solving specific problems or meeting particular requirements identified during persona creation.

A Case Study: How User Personas Helped Increase Sales

Consider an example where a start-up, offering premium organic skincare products, saw their sales skyrocket after implementing user personas into their marketing strategy. Initially, they grouped all women between ages 20 to 45 as a single target audience. However, after conducting detailed market research, they identified two dominant user personas - 'Health-conscious Hannah' and 'Luxury-loving Laura'. Hannah represented young professionals seeking chemical-free alternatives for skincare due to health concerns, while Laura represented affluent women who valued luxury and exclusivity in the products they used.

With these defined personas in place, the start-up revamped its marketing approach. Simple product descriptions were transformed into narratives of 'pampering oneself' for Laura and 'choosing a healthier lifestyle' for Hannah. As a result, customers felt understood and catered to, which translated into higher sales and customer loyalty.

Thus, defining user personas can be instrumental in understanding your customer's journey and tailoring your brand's narrative accordingly. It helps businesses delve deeper than surface-level customer characteristics and tap into what drives consumer behavior - an understanding integral for success in today's competitive marketplace.

## Value Proposition and Product-Market Fit

Once the target audience is accurately identified through user personas, businesses must next focus on defining their product's value proposition and achieving a strong product-market fit. The term 'product-market fit' refers to the degree to which a product or service corresponds with the exact needs of a specific market segment.

A clear value proposition helps differentiate your business in a saturated marketplace. It can be defined as the unique combination of features and benefits that a product offers, which directly address and resolve customers' pain points. Essentially, it's what makes your potential customers think, "This product is made just for me."

## The Importance of Product-Market Fit

Achieving the right product-market fit isn't optional; it's a necessity for survival in today's competitive business landscape. You may have the most innovative product or service but without establishing its relevancy to your target audience, success will remain elusive.

This becomes even more critical for start-ups operating on limited resources where each dollar spent must drive measurable results. Achieving a strong product-market fit ensures that every marketing effort made aligns perfectly with customer needs, maximizing opportunities for growth and returns on investment.

**Adjusting Your Product-Market Fit for Different Stakeholders**

A crucial aspect often overlooked is that while your primary stakeholders are indeed your customers, they aren't the only ones. There can be secondary stakeholders who have an indirect relationship with your product or service including investors, partners, suppliers etc. Therefore, adjusting your product-market fit to appeal to these different stakeholders becomes pertinent. For instance, consider how you might pitch your start-up idea to potential investors. Here, instead of dwelling solely on how the product serves customer needs, you need to emphasize the potential returns, scalable business model, or your team's unique capabilities. In contrast, marketers would want to hear how your product can capture greater market share, while suppliers might be more interested in knowing about production and inventory plans.

**Understanding What Customers Find Value In**

To craft a compelling value proposition and ensure a strong product-market fit, one must delve into understanding what customers truly find valuable. This involves segmenting the benefits your product offers into two categories – functional and emotional benefits.

Functional benefits are tangible outcomes of using your product - for example, an acne cream promising clear skin in two weeks. Emotional benefits on the other hand are intangible outcomes that make customers feel good after purchase - such as feeling confident with clear skin. Both these aspects work together in creating a value proposition that resonates strongly with your target customer persona.

**Mapping Competition through Competitive Analysis**

Achieving product-market fit doesn't occur in isolation; it necessitates keeping a pulse on competitive trends too. Conducting a competitive analysis helps identify where you stand in relation to competitors and how to strategically position your product. It provides insights into competitor strategies, strengths and weaknesses thus enabling businesses to carve out their own unique space in the market.

Thereby, combining competitor wisdom with customer insights paints a holistic picture crucial for achieving optimal product-market fit. As a result, not only do start-ups set themselves up for sustainable growth but they also create stronger relationships with their customers, driving long-term success.

**Investor Appeal through Pricing Strategy and Hyper-personalized Marketing**

While a lot of effort goes into understanding the market, defining user personas, and achieving product-market fit, it's equally important to focus on building investor appeal. Investors are not only crucial for providing financial support but also bring in valuable industry knowledge, business connections, and credibility. As such, adjusting your marketing strategy to attract investors is as critical as targeting consumers.

The crux of attracting investors lies in demonstrating the potential for high return on investment. This encompasses showcasing a strong product-market fit, efficient business model, scalable opportunities and a compelling pricing strategy.

**Pricing Your Product Right: Understanding Pricing Analysis and Strategy**

Though often overlooked in favor of design and features, pricing plays a vital role in both the consumer decision-making process and investor appeal. Therefore, an effective pricing strategy is one which not only appeals to your target market but also attracts potential investors by showing profitability.

A comprehensive pricing analysis helps determine the optimum price point for your product or service. It involves studying factors like production costs, market demand, competitor prices, consumer expectations and willingness to pay. A well-executed pricing analysis allows start-ups to find a balance between profitability and customer acceptance.

For instance, if you're selling handmade soap bars at $10 per piece while competitors offer similar quality soap at $5 per piece, obviously there's a mismatch in terms of perceived value.

Unless you can justify why your soap is worth double the price (such as unique ingredients or benefits), customers are unlikely to buy it and investors could be wary about its market success. Thus, nailing down a competitive yet profitable price point adds another layer of attractiveness from an investor's perspective.

**Leveraging Hyper-personalized Marketing Methods**

In today's digital age, hyper-personalization is the key to marketing success. Hyper-personalized marketing involves using collected data to deliver more relevant messages, offers and product recommendations tailored uniquely to each user.

Not only does this strategy improve customer engagement and satisfaction, but it also signifies your start-up's capacity to adapt to modern marketing trends. By collecting and analyzing customer data effectively, you demonstrate that your business is able to understand its customers on a granular level – an attribute which is highly appealing for investors.

Additionally, hyper-personalized marketing strategies have been shown to dramatically increase conversion rates and customer loyalty. Both of these aspects are attractive for investors as they provide clear evidence of business growth potential.

Therefore, focusing on understanding your pricing strategy and incorporating hyper-personalized marketing methods not only elevates your start-up's appeal among consumers but also plays an integral part in securing investor interest.

# Intellectual Property
# and Competitive Edge

Welcome to Chapter 17 of our series, where we delve into the fascinating world of Intellectual Property and its role in providing a competitive edge to businesses. In this chapter, we explore how Intellectual Property safeguards creations, fuels growth, and gives businesses an undeniable advantage in the market.

Intellectual Property, often abbreviated as IP, refers to a broad spectrum of intangible assets that businesses rely on for success. These assets include trademarks, copyrights, patents, and trade secrets, which are all vital elements in safeguarding creations and fueling growth in today's global business landscape.

By understanding and effectively utilizing Intellectual Property, businesses can establish a solid foundation and a distinctive brand identity. It allows them to protect their innovative ideas, creative works, and confidential information, ultimately giving them a competitive edge over their counterparts.

In the upcoming sections, we will explore the various aspects of Intellectual Property, including trademarks, patents, copyrights, and trade secrets. Additionally, we will delve into the importance of brand selection, federal registration, and the enforcement of Intellectual Property rights.

So, join us as we uncover the power of Intellectual Property in safeguarding creations, fueling growth, and providing businesses with a remarkable competitive edge in the modern marketplace.

**Introduction to Intellectual Property (IP) for Foreign Investors**

Foreign investors play a crucial role in the global economy, driving innovation and contributing to economic growth. To thrive in the international market, it is essential for these investors to understand and protect their Intellectual Property (IP) assets.

Intellectual Property refers to intangible creations of the human intellect, such as inventions, artistic works, and unique business processes. For foreign investors, IP assets encompass a range of valuable elements, including trademarks, copyrights, patents, and trade secrets.

Trademarks are distinctive signs that identify and distinguish goods or services in the market. They can be in the form of logos, words, or even sounds. By registering trademarks, foreign investors can establish brand recognition and prevent others from using similar marks that may cause confusion among consumers.

Copyrights protect original creative works such as literature, music, and art. By obtaining copyright protection, foreign investors ensure that their works are exclusively attributed to them, giving them the right to reproduce, distribute, and display their creations.

Patents are granted to inventors for their new inventions, providing them with exclusive rights to commercially exploit their innovative ideas. By obtaining a patent, foreign investors can prevent others from making, using, or selling their patented inventions without permission.

Trade secrets refer to confidential business information that gives a foreign investor a competitive advantage. These can include manufacturing processes, customer lists, or marketing strategies. Protecting trade secrets ensures that competitors cannot gain access to valuable proprietary information.

For foreign investors, safeguarding these IP assets is crucial for maintaining a competitive edge in the international market. Without adequate protection, their innovations can be easily copied or misappropriated, leading to potential financial losses and damage to their brand reputation.

In the following sections of this book, we will explore in more detail the different types of Intellectual Property and the importance of protecting and enforcing these assets for foreign investors operating in a globalized economy.

## Trademarks and Servicemarks

Establishing a strong brand identity is crucial for businesses, and trademarks and servicemarks play a vital role in this process. These marks serve as valuable assets that differentiate a business's products or services from competitors in the market.

A trademark is used to protect unique names, logos, slogans, or symbols associated with a business. On the other hand, a servicemark is specifically designed to protect and identify services offered by a business rather than tangible products.

Protecting trademarks and servicemarks is essential to maintain brand integrity and prevent confusion among consumers. Registering these marks with the appropriate authorities provides federal protection and establishes legal rights to the ownership of the marks.

One of the primary goals of trademark and service mark registration is to avoid the likelihood of confusion among consumers. This likelihood of confusion occurs when a mark is similar or identical to an existing mark in the same industry, leading consumers to believe that the products or services come from the same source.

By obtaining federal protection, businesses can safeguard their trademarks and service marks, ensuring exclusivity and preventing others from using similar marks that may create confusion in the marketplace.

| Benefits of Protecting Trademarks and Servicemarks |
| --- |
| Establishes brand identity and recognition |
| Prevents competitors from using similar marks |
| Builds consumer trust and loyalty |
| Enables legal action against infringers |
| Enhances the value of the business |

## Patents and Trade Secrets

When it comes to safeguarding inventions and confidential information, patents and trade secrets play a vital role in intellectual property protection. Patents grant exclusive rights to the innovator, allowing them to prevent others from making, using, or selling their invention without permission. On the other hand, trade secrets maintain the confidentiality of valuable business information, such as formulas, processes, or customer lists, that provide a competitive advantage.

With patents, innovators can protect their technological advancements and ensure that they have the exclusive ability to capitalize on their inventions. The process of obtaining a patent involves disclosing the invention to the public in exchange for the protection granted by the patent rights. This protection enables inventors to monetize their creations, attract investors, and fuel further innovation.

Trade secrets, on the other hand, rely on maintaining the secrecy of valuable proprietary information. Unlike patents, trade secrets don't require disclosure to the public. Instead, businesses must take reasonable steps to keep the information confidential, such as implementing strict access controls, non-disclosure agreements, and other security measures.

Both patents and trade secrets provide different avenues for intellectual property protection, depending on the nature of the invention or information being safeguarded. It is essential for businesses to evaluate their options and determine the most suitable form of protection to ensure the longevity and exclusivity of their assets.

## Copyrights

Copyrights are an essential aspect of protecting original creative works, providing creators with exclusive rights and ensuring copyright protection. These rights extend to a wide range of creative works, including literature, music, art, films, and software.

When an individual or entity holds copyright, they have the exclusive right to reproduce, distribute, display, perform, and create derivative works based on their copyrighted material. This exclusive control allows creators to monetize their works and maintain ownership over their creations.

To gain copyright protection, a work must be original and fixed in a tangible medium, such as a book, recording, or painting. Registration with the U.S. Copyright Office is not required for copyright protection, as copyright is automatically granted upon creation. However, registration provides additional benefits, including the ability to pursue legal action against infringement and seek statutory damages.

Infringement of copyrights occurs when someone uses, copies, or distributes copyrighted material without obtaining permission from the copyright holder. Copyright infringement can result in legal consequences, including injunctions, monetary damages, and the seizure of infringing copies.

*Table: Types of Creative Works Protected by Copyrights*

| Types of Works | Description |
|---|---|
| Literary Works | Includes novels, poems, short stories, books, and other written works. |
| Musical Works | Compositions with or without lyrics, including songs and instrumental pieces. |
| Artistic Works | Paintings, drawings, sculptures, photographs, and other visual arts. |
| Films and Audiovisual Works | Movies, television shows, documentaries, and other audiovisual productions. |
| Architectural Works | Architectural designs, building plans, and structures. |
| Software and Computer Programs | Code, algorithms, and software applications. |

Copyright protection is essential for creators to monetize their works and maintain control over their creative endeavors. By understanding their rights and taking necessary measures to protect their copyrights, creators can ensure their exclusive rights are upheld and their works are safeguarded for future generations.

## Importance of Trademark Selection and Clearance

In today's competitive business landscape, selecting a distinctive and legally protectable trademark is paramount. A strong trademark not only helps you stand out from the crowd but also serves as a vital tool for brand recognition and customer loyalty. However, choosing the right trademark requires careful consideration and thorough research to ensure its availability and avoid potential conflicts.

*Trademark selection* involves brainstorming and identifying unique and memorable words, symbols, or designs that accurately represent your brand's identity and values. It is crucial to select a trademark that resonates with your target audience and effectively communicates your brand's message. Additionally, trademarks should be legally protectable to safeguard your brand's reputation and prevent potential infringement issues.

Once you have narrowed down your choices, the next critical step is *trademark clearance*. This involves conducting comprehensive searches to determine the availability of your chosen trademark and evaluate the likelihood of confusion with existing trademarks. By performing trademark clearance, you can minimize the risk of infringing upon someone else's trademark and facing costly legal consequences.

The *likelihood of confusion*, a key concept in trademark law, refers to the likelihood that consumers may be confused or deceived by similar trademarks. Evaluating the likelihood of confusion is crucial to protect your brand's integrity and prevent consumer confusion, as it can negatively impact your business's reputation and market position.

Investing time and resources into trademark selection and clearance not only helps protect your brand but also ensures that you are building a strong foundation for your business's long-term success. By securing a distinctive and legally protectable trademark, you establish a unique presence in the market and gain a competitive edge over your rivals.

In conclusion, trademark selection and clearance are critical steps in brand protection. By choosing a distinctive and legally protectable trademark, conducting thorough searches, and evaluating the likelihood of confusion, you can safeguard your brand's reputation, establish a strong brand identity, and position your business for sustained growth.

## Federal Registration of Trademarks

Registering trademarks with the US Patent and Trademark Office (USPTO) is a crucial step in securing national protection for your brand. The USPTO is responsible for granting federal registration of trademarks, ensuring legal rights and trademark protection under the Lanham Act.

The Lanham Act, also known as the Trademark Act of 1946, governs trademark registration and enforcement in the United States. It establishes the legal framework for protecting trademarks and provides remedies for infringement.

By obtaining federal registration, trademark owners enjoy exclusive rights to use their mark in connection with the goods or services listed in their registration. This significantly strengthens their legal position in defending their brand against unauthorized use by others.

The benefits of federal registration include:

- *Nationwide Protection:* Federal registration provides trademark owners with protection across all 50 states, ensuring broad territorial rights.
- *Presumption of Validity:* A federally registered trademark carries a presumption of validity, making it easier to establish rights and enforce them if necessary.
- *Trademark Symbol:* Registered trademarks can use the ® symbol, notifying others that the mark is federally protected.
- *Enhanced Enforcement:* Federal registration grants access to federal courts, allowing trademark owners to seek legal remedies and damages in case of infringement.

## Trademark Registration Process

**The process of federal trademark registration involves several steps:**

1. Filing an Application: Submit a trademark application to the USPTO, providing details about the mark, its goods or services, and evidence of its use in commerce, if available.
2. Examination: The USPTO examines the application to ensure compliance with statutory requirements and assesses the mark's distinctiveness.
3. Publication: If the application meets all requirements, it is published in the Official Gazette to allow third parties to challenge the registration.
4. Registration: If no opposition is filed or successfully resolved, the USPTO registers the trademark, granting nationwide protection and legal rights to the owner.

**Trademark Registration Statistics**

| Year | Number of Applications | Number of Registrations |
|------|------------------------|-------------------------|
| 2020 | 476,797 | 352,016 |
| 2019 | 462,373 | 326,934 |
| 2018 | 440,769 | 323,313 |

## Intellectual Property Protection in the Digital Environment

In today's digital world, protecting intellectual property (IP) has become more crucial than ever. The rapid advancement of technology and the widespread accessibility of information online have created new challenges for copyright enforcement and combating online infringement. To address these concerns, the Digital Millennium Copyright Act (DMCA) was established in 1998.

The DMCA provides mechanisms for the enforcement of copyright in the digital space. It offers a framework for copyright holders to fight against online infringement, protect their creative works, and maintain control over their intellectual property. The DMCA includes provisions for notice and takedown procedures, copyright safe harbors, and digital rights management.

Under the DMCA, copyright owners can send a takedown notice to website hosts or internet service providers (ISPs) when they discover infringing content online. The website or ISP is then required to remove the copyrighted material promptly. This process allows copyright holders to take action against online infringement efficiently.

Moreover, the DMCA offers protection for online platforms and service providers through its safe harbor provisions. These provisions shield online service providers from liability for copyright infringement committed by their users, as long as the platforms comply with certain requirements, such as implementing a notice and takedown system.

To protect their intellectual property in the digital environment effectively, copyright holders must familiarize themselves with the DMCA and its provisions. By understanding the DMCA's mechanisms, creators can take proactive steps to enforce their copyright and ensure their work is protected from unauthorized use in the digital realm.

## DMCA Notice and Takedown Process

| Step | Description |
|------|-------------|
| 1 | The copyright holder discovers infringing content online. |
| 2 | The copyright holder sends a takedown notice to the website host or ISP. |
| 3 | The website host or ISP removes the infringing content promptly. |
| 4 | If the alleged infringer believes the takedown was unwarranted, they can file a counter-notice. |
| 5 | If a counter-notice is filed, the copyright holder can decide to pursue legal action. |

The DMCA plays a vital role in promoting copyright enforcement and protecting intellectual property rights in the digital environment. By leveraging the provisions of this legislation, copyright holders can safeguard their creative works and ensure their continued success in the online world.

## Enforcement of Intellectual Property Rights

Proper enforcement of intellectual property rights is essential to combat infringement and protect the value of intellectual property. When unauthorized use or copying of IP occurs, legal remedies can be pursued to ensure the rights and interests of IP owners are upheld.

## Cease and Desist Letters

Cease and desist letters are a common initial step taken by IP owners to put an infringer on notice. These letters typically outline the specific infringing actions and demand the immediate cessation of such activities to avoid further legal consequences.

## Infringement Damages

In cases where infringement has already occurred, IP owners can seek monetary damages to compensate for the harm caused. These damages may include actual damages, which calculate the direct economic loss suffered by the IP owner, and statutory damages, which provide a predetermined amount set by law.

It is important to note that damages awarded for infringement typically consider factors such as the nature of the IP, the extent of the infringement, and any profits gained by the infringer as a result.

## Legal Remedies

Beyond cease and desist letters and monetary damages, there are various legal remedies available to enforce intellectual property rights. These remedies may include injunctive relief, which seeks court orders to stop the infringing activities immediately, as well as the seizure, impoundment, or destruction of infringing products.

Moreover, in some cases, criminal action can be pursued against willful and deliberate infringers, leading to fines and potential imprisonment. These legal actions serve as impactful deterrents and reinforce the importance of respecting intellectual property rights.

| Legal Remedy | Description |
|---|---|
| Injunctive Relief | Court orders to halt infringing activities |
| Seizure, Impoundment, or Destruction | Removal or destruction of infringing products |
| Criminal Action | Prosecution of willful and deliberate infringers |

IP enforcement plays a vital role in maintaining the integrity of intellectual property rights and protecting the innovation and creativity that fuels progress in various industries.

## International Intellectual Property Protection

Protecting intellectual property (IP) globally is crucial for businesses operating in the international market. Through international treaties and organizations like the Paris Convention and the World Intellectual Property Organization (WIPO), global trademark protection and harmonization of rights across borders are facilitated.

The Paris Convention, established in 1883, is one of the oldest and most influential international treaties on intellectual property. Its primary goal is to promote and protect industrial property, including trademarks, patents, and industrial designs. The convention provides a framework for cooperation among member countries, enabling businesses to seek protection for their IP in multiple jurisdictions.

WIPO, a specialized agency of the United Nations, plays a key role in fostering global intellectual property protection. It administers various international treaties and provides a platform for cooperation and information exchange between member states. WIPO's services, such as the Patent Cooperation Treaty (PCT) and the Madrid System for international trademark registration, simplify the process of obtaining IP protection in multiple countries.

Global trademark protection ensures that businesses can establish their brand identity and prevent unauthorized use or infringement worldwide. By securing trademark rights through international mechanisms, businesses can expand their market reach and maintain a consistent brand presence across different jurisdictions.

**Figure 10.1: Paris Convention Member Countries**

| Country | Year of Accession |
|---|---|
| United States | 1887 |
| United Kingdom | 1884 |
| Germany | 1883 |
| France | 1883 |
| Japan | 1899 |
| Australia | 1904 |

Table 10.1 showcases a few member countries of the Paris Convention and their year of accession. The convention's wide membership ensures that businesses can protect their IP in numerous countries and benefit from the harmonized legal framework.

With the support of international treaties and organizations, businesses can navigate the complex landscape of international intellectual property rights and ensure the effective protection of their valuable assets.

## Leveraging Intellectual Property for Business Growth

Intellectual Property (IP) is not only a legal protection for your creations but also a valuable asset that can drive business growth and give you a competitive edge in the market. By strategically leveraging your IP assets, you can unlock new opportunities, generate additional revenue streams, and establish a strong position in your industry.

## IP as an Investment

Just like any other investment, IP can yield long-term benefits for your business. By protecting your innovative ideas, inventions, and unique branding elements, you are essentially creating valuable intangible assets. These assets can attract potential investors, increase your company's valuation, and open doors to collaborations, partnerships, and funding opportunities.

## Enhancing Competitive Edge

Having a well-protected IP portfolio can give your business a significant competitive advantage. It sets you apart from competitors and establishes a barrier to entry, making it harder for others to replicate your products or services. This exclusivity allows you to offer unique value propositions and differentiate yourself in the market, attracting more customers and increasing brand loyalty.

## Licensing IP

One of the most effective ways to monetize your IP assets is through licensing agreements. By granting others the right to use, manufacture, or sell your IP, you can generate revenue streams without having to invest in production, marketing, or distribution. Licensing agreements can be tailored to your business goals, allowing you to reach new markets, expand your reach, and tap into the expertise and resources of other companies.

## IP Monetization

IP monetization goes beyond licensing and encompasses various strategies for extracting value from your IP assets. This can include selling or leasing your IP, entering into joint ventures or strategic partnerships, or even utilizing your IP as collateral for financing. By monetizing your IP, you can diversify your revenue streams, maximize the return on your investments, and fuel further growth and innovation.

In summary, leveraging intellectual property as an investment and competitive edge can propel your business forward. Through licensing and IP monetization strategies, you can unlock the full potential of your IP assets and drive business growth in a dynamic and evolving market.

| Benefits of Leveraging IP for Business Growth |
|---|
| |

| |
|---|
| **Increased Valuation:** Protecting your IP assets can attract investors and increase your company's overall valuation. |
| **Market Differentiation:** Well-protected IP sets you apart from competitors, making it harder for them to replicate your products or services. |
| **Diversified Revenue Streams:** Licensing, selling, or leasing your IP allows you to generate additional income without significant investments. |
| **Partnerships and Collaborations:** IP can be leveraged to forge strategic partnerships and collaborations, enhancing your business capabilities. |
| **Maximized ROI:** Monetizing your IP assets helps you extract the maximum value from your investments, funding further growth and innovation. |

Intellectual Property (IP) is a powerful tool that businesses can use to protect their creations, stimulate growth, and gain a competitive edge in the market. By securing trademarks, copyrights, patents, and trade secrets, companies can safeguard their unique ideas and innovations, establishing a strong brand identity.

Effective IP management is essential for success in the modern economy. By registering trademarks and obtaining patents, businesses can ensure legal protection and prevent confusion among consumers. Copyrights give creators exclusive rights over their artistic works, enabling them to take action against infringement.

Furthermore, intellectual property can be leveraged as an investment, fueling business growth and generating additional revenue streams. Through licensing agreements and IP monetization, companies can profit from their valuable intangible assets. This not only strengthens their competitive edge but also fosters innovation and creativity.

In conclusion, Intellectual Property is a critical component of any business strategy. By recognizing the importance of IP protection and leveraging its assets, a company can establish itself as a leader in its industry, drive growth, and stay ahead of the competition.

# Financial Projections
# and Realism

Welcome to Chapter 18 of our book, where we delve into the importance of financial projections and the role they play in making sound financial decisions. In today's fast-paced business environment, realistic financial planning is crucial for success. It requires careful consideration of key assumptions, such as sales forecasts, cost of production, and cash flow planning.

Accurate financial projections enable businesses to shape their investments, drive strategic decision-making, and create a solid foundation for growth. Whether you're a startup or an established company expanding your operations, understanding the financial health of your business is essential.

By developing realistic financial models and considering various scenarios, you can determine the feasibility of your business, attract potential investors, and satisfy the needs of lenders. Additionally, financial projections provide valuable insights for monitoring your business's financial performance and making informed investment decisions.

So, join us as we explore the fascinating world of financial projections and discover how they can guide your path to success. Let's dive in and unlock the key to sound financial planning and decision-making!

The Purpose of Good Financial Planning

Good financial planning is essential for the success and longevity of a business. It serves the purpose of determining the feasibility and sustainability of a business venture, ensuring that it can thrive in the long term.

One of the key aspects of good financial planning is conducting thorough market research. This involves analyzing the target market, understanding customer needs and preferences, and identifying potential competitors. By gathering this information, businesses can make informed decisions about their product/service offerings and pricing strategies, increasing their chances of success.

Accurate cost estimates are another crucial component of good financial planning. Businesses need to understand the costs associated with their operations, including production costs, overhead expenses, and marketing expenses. This allows them to set realistic prices for their products/services and ensure that they can cover their costs while maintaining a competitive edge.

Financial forecasts are also an integral part of good financial planning. These forecasts provide businesses with a clear picture of their future financial performance, including projected revenues, expenses, and cash flow. They help businesses to plan and allocate resources effectively, make informed investment decisions, and attract investors and lenders.

In summary, good financial planning is essential for business feasibility and sustainability. Through market research, accurate cost estimates, and financial forecasting, businesses can make informed decisions, attract investment, and position themselves for long-term success.

Understanding Start-up Costs

Start-up costs are the expenses required to get a business off the ground or implement expansion plans. These costs encompass various aspects such as equipment, inventory, marketing, employee salaries, permits, licenses, and more. Properly estimating and managing start-up costs is vital for the success of both start-up companies and businesses looking to expand their operations.

In order to effectively plan for start-up costs, it is essential to gather data from potential suppliers and service providers. This allows entrepreneurs to determine accurate cost estimates for their various business needs. Additionally, understanding anticipated borrowing expenses and terms is crucial for making informed decisions about capital funding.

Feasibility assessments play a key role in understanding start-up costs. By conducting thorough assessments, entrepreneurs can determine if their business plan is financially viable. Feasibility assessments involve evaluating market opportunities, analyzing potential revenue streams, assessing competition, and identifying potential risks and challenges.

One effective way to organize and analyze start-up costs is through the use of a start-up cost worksheet. This worksheet allows entrepreneurs to categorize and track their expenses, ensuring that all essential cost elements are accounted for. By diligently tracking their start-up costs, entrepreneurs can make informed decisions, identify areas where cost savings can be achieved, and present a comprehensive financial picture to potential investors or lenders.

**Sample Start-up Cost Worksheet:**

| Expense Category | Estimated Cost |
| --- | --- |
| Equipment | $10,000 |
| Inventory | $5,000 |
| Marketing | $3,000 |
| Salaries | $20,000 |
| Permits and Licenses | $2,000 |
| Legal and Accounting Fees | $2,500 |
| Technology and Software | $4,000 |
| Contingency Fund | $5,000 |
| **Total** | **$51,500** |

By conducting thorough feasibility assessments and effectively managing start-up costs, entrepreneurs can set their businesses up for success. Understanding the financial requirements and ensuring adequate capital funding contributes to a strong foundation for growth and profitability.

### Key Assumptions in Financial Projections

When creating financial projections, it is crucial to establish key assumptions that form the foundation of the forecasts. These assumptions play a vital role in determining the accuracy and reliability of financial forecasts, such as balance sheets, income statements, cash flow plans, and business plans.

The key assumptions typically encompass various aspects of the business, including sales projections, cost of production, and general administrative expenses.

### Sales Projections

Accurate sales projections are essential for estimating revenue and determining the financial feasibility of a business. These projections consider market conditions, customer demand, competitive landscape, and marketing strategies. By analyzing historical sales data and market trends, businesses can make informed assumptions about future sales volumes.

### Cost of Production

The cost of production is a critical assumption in financial projections, as it directly impacts the profitability of a business. It includes expenses related to raw materials, labor, manufacturing processes, and overhead costs. Accurate estimation of the cost of production enables businesses to determine appropriate pricing strategies and assess the feasibility of product or service offerings.

## General Administrative Expenses

General administrative expenses encompass various operating costs that do not directly contribute to the cost of production. These expenses typically include salaries, rent, utilities, insurance, marketing, and other overhead costs. By accurately estimating these expenses, businesses can project their operational costs and evaluate their financial performance.

By effectively incorporating these key assumptions into financial projections, businesses can create a comprehensive financial forecast that guides their decision-making process and supports their strategic goals.

| Key Assumptions | Financial Forecasts |
| --- | --- |
| Sales Projections | Estimate revenue and determine financial feasibility |
| Cost of Production | Impact profitability and assess feasibility of offerings |
| General Administrative Expenses | Project operational costs and evaluate financial performance |

### The Impact of Financial Projections on Investment Decisions

Financial projections play a crucial role in guiding investment decisions for businesses. They provide valuable information that helps attract potential investors and satisfy the requirements of lenders. Furthermore, financial projections allow businesses to monitor their financial performance and make informed decisions that drive growth and profitability.

When creating financial projections, it is essential to develop realistic and accurate models that reflect the potential outcomes of various investment scenarios. This involves understanding and analyzing financial ratios and metrics to assess the feasibility and profitability of the investment.

By presenting comprehensive financial projections, businesses can demonstrate their potential to generate returns, mitigate risks, and align with the investment objectives of potential investors and lenders.

### Benefits of Financial Projections in Investment Decisions:

1. Attracting Investors: Well-prepared financial projections can help businesses attract investors by showcasing the profitability, growth potential, and financial stability of the investment opportunity.
2. Satisfying Lenders: Financial projections provide lenders with crucial information to assess the borrower's ability to manage debt and generate income, thus satisfying their requirements for loan approval.
3. Monitoring Financial Performance: Financial projections serve as benchmarks for monitoring the actual financial performance of a business against projected figures, enabling timely decision-making and course corrections.
1. Overall, financial projections serve as a roadmap for investment decisions, giving businesses the confidence to pursue growth opportunities and make informed choices that drive financial success.

| | Benefits |
| --- | --- |
| Attracting Investors | Showcasing profitability and growth potential |
| Satisfying Lenders | Demonstrating ability to manage debt |
| Monitoring Financial Performance | Benchmarking actual performance against projections |

### Building Financial Knowledge and Decision-Making Skills

Building financial knowledge and decision-making skills is crucial for individuals to make sound financial choices. These skills develop during adolescence and young adulthood and enable individuals to understand advanced financial concepts, manage credit and debt wisely, and seek credible financial information.

Financial knowledge empowers individuals to navigate complex financial landscapes, make informed decisions, and achieve financial well-being. It equips them with the understanding of financial products, services, and markets, allowing them to identify opportunities and mitigate risks.

Decision-making skills play a vital role in financial well-being. These skills involve critical thinking, analyzing financial data, evaluating risks and rewards, setting financial goals, and creating effective financial plans. Decision-making skills enable individuals to allocate resources wisely, prioritize financial goals, and adapt to changing economic conditions.

It is essential to develop financial knowledge and decision-making skills early on in life. Schools, colleges, and universities play a crucial role in imparting financial education. By incorporating financial literacy programs into the curriculum, educational institutions can equip students with the necessary skills to make informed financial decisions.

## The Benefits of Financial Knowledge and Decision-Making Skills

**Gaining financial knowledge and honing decision-making skills offer numerous benefits:**

- *Improved Financial Decision-Making:* Individuals with strong financial knowledge and decision-making skills are better equipped to make wise investment choices, manage debt effectively, and plan for a financially secure future.

- *Financial Independence:* Understanding personal finance and developing decision-making skills empowers individuals to take control of their financial lives, reducing reliance on others and fostering independence.

- *Increased Financial Well-being:* Building financial knowledge and decision-making skills leads to better financial outcomes, improved financial stability, and enhanced overall well-being.

- *Protection Against Fraud:* Financially savvy individuals are better equipped to identify and avoid financial scams and fraudulent schemes, protecting their assets and financial security.

By investing in financial education and developing decision-making skills, individuals can enhance their financial knowledge, make informed choices, and ultimately achieve greater financial well-being.

## Teaching Financial Knowledge and Decision-Making Skills

Schools play a crucial role in equipping students with the necessary financial knowledge and decision-making skills to navigate their future financial lives. By implementing effective instructional strategies, educators can empower students to develop good financial behaviors and make informed financial choices. Let's explore some of the instructional strategies that can be employed to foster financial competence.

## Competency-Based Learning

Competency-based learning is an instructional approach that focuses on students mastering specific skills and knowledge. In the context of financial education, this method allows students to progress at their own pace, ensuring they grasp foundational concepts before advancing to more complex topics. By emphasizing hands-on experiences and practical applications, students can develop a solid understanding of financial concepts and how to apply them in real-life scenarios.

## Direct Instruction

Direct instruction involves a systematic and explicit teaching approach. With this strategy, educators convey financial concepts and principles directly to students, providing step-by-step explanations and opportunities for practice. By using clear and concise language, educators can help students grasp complex financial concepts more easily.

## Personalized Instruction

Personalized instruction tailors the learning experience to meet the individual needs and interests of each student. In financial education, this can involve adapting the curriculum to address specific financial goals or challenges that students may face. By incorporating real-world examples and relating financial concepts to students' lives, educators can enhance engagement and relevance.

## Project-Based Learning

Project-based learning immerses students in real-world financial scenarios, where they apply their knowledge and skills to solve problems or complete projects. By working collaboratively and independently, students develop critical thinking, problem-solving, and decision-making skills. Project-based learning also helps students understand the financial implications of their choices and the importance of making informed decisions.

## Simulations

Simulations offer a realistic and interactive learning experience that replicates financial situations, such as managing a budget, investing, or starting a business. By immersing students in these simulations, educators provide a safe environment for students to practice financial decision-making and experience the potential consequences of their choices. This hands-on approach helps students develop confidence and competence in managing their finances.

Effective instructional strategies play a vital role in teaching financial knowledge and decision-making skills to students. By incorporating competency-based learning, direct instruction, personalized instruction, project-based learning, and simulations, schools can empower students to become financially literate individuals prepared for future financial success.

| Instructional Strategies | Description |
| --- | --- |
| Competency-Based Learning | An instructional approach focused on students mastering specific skills and knowledge at their own pace through hands-on experiences and practical applications. |
| Direct Instruction | A systematic and explicit teaching approach where educators provide step-by-step explanations and practice opportunities to help students grasp complex financial concepts. |
| Personalized Instruction | Tailoring the learning experience to meet individual students' needs and interests by relating financial concepts to their lives and goals. |
| Project-Based Learning | Involves students in real-world financial scenarios, where they apply their knowledge and skills to solve problems or complete projects, enhancing critical thinking and decision-making skills. |
| Simulations | Replicating financial situations through interactive simulations, providing a safe environment for students to practice financial decision-making and experience consequences. |

## Servicing Non-Performing Loans

In the process of managing non-performing loans, prompt and aggressive action is crucial to help borrowers bring their accounts current. Servicing non-performing loans involves various collection efforts, meticulous record-keeping, following industry practices, and exploring loss mitigation options. It is essential to maintain accurate servicing logs and foster cooperation with borrowers throughout the process to achieve the best possible outcomes.

## The Collection Efforts Process

When a loan becomes non-performing, effective collection efforts are vital to encourage borrowers to fulfill their financial obligations. These efforts often include:

| Collection Efforts | Description |
|---|---|
| **Initial Contact** | Reaching out to borrowers to discuss payment alternatives and assess the borrower's financial situation. |
| **Notification to Credit Repositories** | Notifying credit reporting agencies about the delinquent loan to reflect the borrower's failure to meet their repayment obligations. |
| **Issuing Certified Letters** | Sending formal notification letters via certified mail to document the servicer's attempts to collect payments and the borrower's failure to respond. |
| **Property Inspection** | Conducting property inspections to evaluate its condition and assess its value as part of the collection process. |

## Loss Mitigation Options

Successfully mitigating losses in non-performing loans requires exploring various options to assist borrowers in resolving their default situations. Some common loss mitigation measures include:

| Loss Mitigation Options | Description |
|---|---|
| Loan Modifications | Modifying the loan terms, such as adjusting interest rates, extending the loan term, or reducing the principal balance, to make it more affordable for borrowers. |
| Repayment Plans | Creating a structured repayment plan that allows borrowers to catch up on missed payments over a specified period while keeping up with their regular mortgage obligations. |
| Forbearance | Temporarily suspending or reducing mortgage payments for borrowers facing short-term financial difficulties while they regain their financial stability. |
| Foreclosure Prevention Measures | Taking proactive steps such as offering foreclosure counseling and assistance programs to help borrowers avoid the possibility of foreclosure. |

By implementing these loss mitigation options, servicers aim to give borrowers an opportunity to overcome financial challenges, ensure borrower satisfaction, and protect the interests of both borrowers and lenders.

## Collection Efforts and Requirements

When a borrower's account becomes past due, it is crucial for the servicer to initiate collection efforts to address the payment delinquency. These collection efforts aim to resolve the outstanding balance and bring the account current. In order to ensure compliance with industry standards and regulatory requirements, servicers must follow specific minimum requirements and adhere to certain practices.

The first step in the collection process is the initial contact with the borrower. This contact may be made via phone call, email, or written communication, depending on the servicer's preferred method of communication. The purpose of this initial contact is to inform the borrower about the delinquency, discuss potential solutions, and establish open lines of communication.

Another essential requirement in the collection efforts is notifying credit repositories about the delinquent account. By reporting the delinquency to the credit bureaus, the servicer ensures that the borrower's credit history reflects the outstanding payment. This reporting not only serves as a record of the borrower's payment behavior but may also have consequences on their credit score and future creditworthiness.

In addition to the initial contact and credit reporting, servicers are typically required to send certified letters to the borrower. These letters serve as formal notices to inform the borrower about the delinquency, emphasize the importance of resolving the outstanding balance, and provide a deadline for payment or response. Certified letters provide a documented record of communication and can be used as evidence if further action becomes necessary.

Furthermore, as part of the collection efforts, servicers may need to inspect the property associated with the delinquent account. Property inspections help servicers assess the borrower's financial situation, validate occupancy status, and gather information that may inform subsequent actions. Property inspections should be conducted in compliance with applicable laws to protect the borrower's rights and ensure fair treatment.

Throughout the collection process, it is crucial for servicers to maintain accurate records of all collection efforts. These records should include details of the initial contact, copies of correspondence, documentation of credit reporting, and records of property inspections. Maintaining comprehensive and organized collection records not only helps servicers monitor the progress of the collection efforts but also ensures compliance with legal and regulatory requirements.

Fulfilling the documentation requirements is vital for servicers to demonstrate their compliance with industry standards and regulations. Inadequate or incomplete documentation may result in regulatory penalties, legal challenges, or a negative impact on the servicer's reputation. By fulfilling documentation requirements, servicers can instill confidence in borrowers, fulfill their legal obligations, and effectively manage the collection process.

Collection Efforts and Requirements Summary:

The table below summarizes the minimum collection efforts and requirements that servicers must undertake when a borrower's account becomes past due:

| Collection Effort/Requirement | Description |
|---|---|
| Initial Contact | Contacting the borrower to discuss the delinquency and explore potential solutions. |
| Credit Reporting | Reporting the delinquent account to credit repositories to reflect the outstanding balance on the borrower's credit history. |
| Certified Letters | Sending formal notices to the borrower via certified mail to inform them of the delinquency, emphasize the importance of resolving the balance, and provide a deadline for payment or response. |
| Property Inspections | Conducting inspections of the property associated with the delinquent account to assess the borrower's financial situation and validate occupancy status. |
| Record Keeping | Maintaining comprehensive and organized records of all collection efforts, including initial contact, correspondence, credit reporting, and property inspections. |
| Fulfilling Documentation Requirements | Ensuring compliance with documentation requirements to demonstrate adherence to industry standards and regulatory obligations. |

**Loss Mitigation Options**

In cases where borrowers find themselves in default situations and are unable to make their mortgage payments, servicers offer a range of loss mitigation options to assist them. These options aim to help borrowers resolve their financial difficulties and avoid foreclosure. Here are some common loss mitigation options:

- *Loan modifications:* This option involves modifying the terms of the existing loan to make it more affordable for the borrower. It can include reducing the interest rate, extending the loan term, or forgiving a portion of the principal balance.
- *Repayment plans:* Under a repayment plan, the borrower agrees to make higher monthly payments for a certain period of time to catch up on the missed payments and bring the loan current.
- *Forbearance:* In situations where the borrower is experiencing temporary financial hardship, the servicer may grant a forbearance, allowing the borrower to temporarily suspend or reduce their mortgage payments until they can get back on their feet.

These loss mitigation options aim to provide mortgage assistance to borrowers facing default situations, helping them find a viable solution and avoid the devastating consequences of foreclosure. By working closely with servicers and exploring these options, borrowers can take steps towards regaining control of their financial situation.

This chapter has highlighted the critical role of realistic financial planning in making sound business decisions. By understanding key assumptions and creating accurate financial projections, you will be better equipped to attract investors, satisfy lenders, and drive the success of your business.

Furthermore, building your financial knowledge and decision-making skills is crucial for making informed choices. Whether you're an individual seeking financial well-being or a business owner looking to drive sustainable growth, developing these skills will empower you to navigate complex financial landscapes with confidence.

Lastly, effective loan servicing and loss mitigation are essential for managing non-performing loans and avoiding financial pitfalls. By taking prompt action, maintaining accurate records, and exploring loss mitigation options, you can minimize the impact of defaults and ensure the financial stability of your business.

Chapter 19

# Social Responsibility and Corporate Ethics

Welcome to Chapter 19 of our module, where we delve into the fascinating realm of social responsibility and corporate ethics. In today's complex business environment, it is essential for organizations to consider not only their financial success but also the impact of their actions on stakeholders and society as a whole.

Corporate ethics and social responsibility have become increasingly significant as the public demands higher ethical standards from businesses. People want to support companies that prioritize values such as integrity, honesty, and fairness. The decisions businesses make about doing the "right thing" can have profound consequences for all parties involved, including stakeholders, society, and the very reputation of the company itself.

This chapter explores various aspects related to corporate ethics, including ethical and legal behavior, ethical challenges, and levels of social responsibility. We will also dive into the concept of creating shared value, the importance of emotional intelligence, and the link between business communication and social responsibility.

So, whether you're an aspiring business professional or a seasoned veteran, join us on this journey to explore the intricate relationship between corporate ethics, social responsibility, and successful investment strategies. Let's discover how businesses can thrive by making ethical decisions that positively impact society.

## Ethical and Legal Behavior

Standards of ethical and legal behavior are intertwined but come from different sources. Legality is determined by legislation or case law, while ethics investigates the best way for people to live and determines right or wrong actions in specific circumstances.

Ethical behavior goes beyond what is legally required, focusing on concepts such as *good and evil*, *right and wrong*, and *justice and crime*. It delves into the complexities of human morality, bringing a deeper understanding of the impact our actions have on ourselves and others.

Businesses and organizations have a responsibility to uphold both ethical and legal behavior. While the law provides a framework for acceptable conduct, ethical standards guide businesses in making choices that align with their values and the welfare of society.

## The Role of Ethical Behavior

Ethical behavior is a reflection of an organization's commitment to doing what is morally right and just. It creates a foundation for relationships, fosters trust, and promotes a positive corporate culture.

When businesses prioritize ethical behavior, they create an environment where employees feel valued and respected. This, in turn, boosts employee morale, productivity, and engagement. Ethical behavior also enhances an organization's reputation, attracting customers and investors who value companies that prioritize social responsibility.

## The Importance of Legal Behavior

Legal behavior ensures that businesses operate within the boundaries set by society. It provides a system of guidelines and consequences for actions that harm others or violate established rules. Complying with laws and regulations is not only a legal obligation but also a moral imperative.

Businesses that prioritize legal behavior demonstrate their commitment to respecting the rights of individuals, protecting the environment, and promoting fairness in business practices. Compliance with laws and regulations also reduces the risk of legal disputes and penalties, safeguarding the company's resources and reputation.

## Cultivating Ethical and Legal Behavior

Cultivating ethical and legal behavior within an organization requires a multi-faceted approach. It starts with clear communication of ethical expectations and the establishment of ethical guidelines. These guidelines should be reinforced through training, regular assessments, and ongoing dialogue.

| Strategies for Cultivating Ethical and Legal Behavior: |
| --- |
| Promote a culture of integrity and accountability |
| Lead by example and exemplify ethical behavior at all levels |
| Provide ongoing ethics training and education |
| Establish procedures for reporting unethical behavior |
| Implement regular assessments and audits of ethical practices |

By fostering an ethical and legal culture, organizations can create an environment where employees are empowered to make ethical decisions and uphold the principles of social responsibility.

## Ethical Challenges

Businesses and their employees often encounter ethical dilemmas in their day-to-day operations. These challenges require careful consideration and decision-making to maintain integrity and ethical behavior. Let's explore some common ethical issues faced by businesses:

## Conflicts of Interest

Conflicts of interest occur when an individual's personal interests or relationships interfere with their professional obligations. This can lead to biased decision-making and compromise the integrity of the business. It's crucial for organizations to have policies in place to identify and address conflicts of interest to ensure fair and unbiased practices.

## Bribes

Bribery is the act of offering, giving, receiving, or soliciting something of value to influence the actions or decisions of an individual in a position of power or authority. Bribes can undermine fair competition, impair ethical standards, and damage the reputation of businesses. To combat bribery, companies should establish clear anti-bribery policies and enforce strict ethical codes of conduct.

## Conflicts of Loyalty

Conflicts of loyalty arise when individuals face competing interests or obligations that may compromise their ethical judgment or loyalty to the organization. Employees may find themselves torn between personal relationships, financial interests, or other external factors that could potentially influence their decision-making. It is essential for organizations to foster a transparent and supportive environment that enables employees to navigate conflicts of loyalty effectively.

## Honesty and Integrity

Honesty and integrity are fundamental principles that businesses must uphold. Acting with honesty means being truthful, transparent, and sincere in all business interactions. It involves delivering accurate information, keeping promises, and maintaining ethical conduct. Maintaining integrity ensures that businesses operate within legal and ethical boundaries, earning the trust and respect of stakeholders.

| Ethical Challenges | Description |
|---|---|
| Conflicts of Interest | Situations where personal interests or relationships influence professional decision-making. |
| Bribes | The act of offering or accepting something valuable to influence actions or decisions. |
| Conflicts of Loyalty | Dilemmas arising from conflicting obligations or interests that may compromise ethical judgment. |
| Honesty and Integrity | The commitment to truthfulness, transparency, and ethical behavior in all business interactions. |

## Corporate Social Responsibility

Corporate social responsibility (CSR) refers to the actions taken by businesses to consider the impact of their decisions on the external environment and the community. It encompasses a range of areas including environmental concerns, poverty alleviation, human rights, and animal rights. Today, businesses are increasingly recognizing the importance of CSR in attracting and retaining both employees and customers.

Stakeholders, including customers, employees, and the general public, are demanding that businesses operate in a socially responsible manner and give back to the community. This not only helps to build a positive reputation but also ensures that businesses are contributing to the betterment of society as a whole.

One area of CSR is environmental concerns, where businesses strive to reduce their carbon footprint, adopt sustainable practices, and protect natural resources. This includes initiatives such as implementing renewable energy sources and reducing waste and pollution.

Another aspect of CSR is poverty alleviation, which involves businesses supporting initiatives that aim to address poverty and social inequality. This can include providing job opportunities, supporting education and skills training programs, and investing in community development projects.

Human rights are also a key focus of CSR. Businesses are expected to uphold human rights principles and ensure fair treatment of employees, suppliers, and customers. This includes promoting diversity and inclusion, ensuring fair wages and safe working conditions, and actively working to prevent human rights abuses within their supply chains.

Clients, customers, and employees are increasingly attracted to businesses that demonstrate a commitment to social responsibility. By incorporating CSR into their operations and decision-making, businesses can position themselves as ethical leaders and make a positive impact on society.

## Levels of Social Responsibility

Social responsibility encompasses various aspects that businesses need to consider in their operations. This section explores the four main levels of social responsibility: economic, legal, ethical, and philanthropic.

## Economic Aspects

At the economic level, businesses prioritize maintaining strong economic interests to stay viable and competitive. They strive to generate profits, create jobs, and contribute to economic growth. Successful businesses prioritize efficiency, innovation, and long-term sustainability to fulfill their economic responsibilities.

## Legal Aspects

Businesses have a fundamental obligation to operate within the boundaries of the law. The legal aspect of social responsibility emphasizes the importance of organizations complying with regulations and meeting their legal obligations. By adhering to legal frameworks, businesses ensure fair and ethical practices in their operations.

## Ethical Aspects

Ethical aspects of social responsibility go beyond legal requirements, focusing on businesses acting in morally and socially responsible ways. Ethical behavior entails making decisions and taking actions that align with principles of fairness, honesty, and integrity. Organizations that prioritize ethical practices build trust, foster positive relationships with stakeholders, and contribute to societal well-being.

## Philanthropic Aspects

Philanthropic aspects of social responsibility involve businesses giving back to society through charitable donations of time, money, and goods. These initiatives aim to make a positive impact on the community, addressing societal needs and enriching the lives of individuals. By engaging in philanthropic activities, organizations fulfill their social responsibilities and contribute to the greater good.

In summary, businesses need to consider multiple levels of social responsibility in their operations. Economic aspects ensure sustainability and growth, while legal aspects promote compliance with regulations. Ethical aspects define the moral compass of organizations, while philanthropic aspects allow businesses to give back to society.

| Levels of Social Responsibility | Description |
|---|---|
| Economic Aspects | Businesses prioritize financial sustainability and economic growth. |
| Legal Aspects | Organizations comply with regulations and meet legal obligations. |
| Ethical Aspects | Businesses make morally and socially responsible decisions. |
| Philanthropic Aspects | Organizations contribute to the community through charitable initiatives. |

## Social Responsibility on the Corporate Level

Companies have faced increasing pressure to behave in a socially responsible manner since the 1960s. Social responsibility on the corporate level means businesses should be concerned about the welfare of society and consider the impact of their actions on society as a whole. However, not all companies fulfill their social responsibility.

One notable example is BP, an energy company that faced accusations of gross negligence for safety violations and environmental harm in the Gulf of Mexico.

| Company | Accusations | Impact |
|---|---|---|
| BP | Gross negligence, safety violations, environmental harm | Damage to marine life, ecosystems, and livelihoods |

The unethical behavior exhibited by BP had severe consequences for the environment and the communities affected. Such instances highlight the ethical expectations of society and the need for companies to act more responsibly.

By fulfilling their social responsibility, businesses can not only avoid legal and reputational repercussions but also contribute positively to society, fostering trust and loyalty among stakeholders.

Next, let's explore social responsibility on the individual level and the role individuals play in upholding ethical standards.

## Social Responsibility on the Individual Level

Individuals within organizations also play a crucial role in driving social responsibility initiatives. The actions and values of individuals can significantly influence the ethical practices and social responsibility efforts undertaken by companies. One exemplary individual who prioritized social responsibility is Anita Roddick, the founder of the Body Shop.

Anita Roddick believed in the importance of environmental friendliness and animal rights, which she incorporated into the products and practices of the Body Shop. Her commitment to these values not only resonated with customers but also set an example for other businesses to prioritize sustainability and ethical sourcing.

Individual social responsibility extends beyond the workplace and encompasses a wide range of actions. It includes engaging in acts of charity, volunteering, supporting social and political issues, and practicing personal ethics such as integrity and honesty in everyday life. By embracing individual social responsibility, people can contribute to the betterment of society and inspire positive change within their communities.

## Creating Shared Value

The concept of creating shared value challenges the belief that social responsibility comes at the cost of profits. In fact, it suggests that companies and the community are closely interconnected, and benefits for one can lead to benefits for the other. This idea was first introduced by Michael E. Porter and Mark R. Kramer in their influential Harvard Business Review book in 2011.

Creating shared value involves identifying and pursuing business opportunities that also have a positive societal impact. It goes beyond traditional corporate social responsibility efforts by integrating the company's core business activities with social and environmental concerns. By doing so, companies can generate economic value while also addressing social challenges.

One example of creating shared value is the initiative taken by some companies to invest in education. By supporting educational programs, these companies not only contribute to the development of the community but also potentially benefit their own workforce. Such investments can enhance the skills and knowledge of potential employees, creating a win-win situation for both the company and the community.

Another example is the adoption of sustainable practices in the supply chain. By considering environmental factors and promoting responsible sourcing and production methods, companies can reduce their carbon footprint and contribute to a healthier planet. This not only benefits society but can also lead to cost savings and operational efficiencies for the company.

| Benefits of Creating Shared Value | Examples |
|---|---|
| Potential for increased profits | Investing in employee training and development |
| Improved brand reputation and customer loyalty | Implementing sustainable supply chain practices |
| Enhanced employee morale and engagement | Supporting community education initiatives |

By creating shared value, companies can align their business goals with societal needs, leading to sustainable growth and long-term success. It is no longer seen as a trade-off between profit and social responsibility, but rather as a way to save money, build trust, and benefit all stakeholders involved.

## The Importance of Emotional Intelligence

Emotional intelligence plays a crucial role in personal and organizational social responsibility. Individuals with high emotional intelligence are more likely to engage in ethical and socially responsible behavior. *Emotional intelligence refers to the ability to recognize, understand, and manage our own emotions and the emotions of others.*

One key aspect of emotional intelligence is *social awareness*. This skill allows individuals to understand and empathize with the emotions and experiences of others. By being socially aware, individuals can better understand how their actions and decisions may impact those around them and society as a whole.

In addition to social awareness, *self-management skills* are also important for practicing social responsibility. Self-management skills involve controlling and directing our own emotions and behaviors in appropriate ways. Individuals with strong self-management skills can make ethical decisions and act in socially responsible ways, even in challenging situations.

Developing emotional intelligence is beneficial for both personal growth and organizational success. For individuals, it leads to improved self-awareness, empathy, and interpersonal relationships. In an organizational context, emotional intelligence contributes to *ethical leadership* and the establishment of a positive work environment.

A *study* conducted by the University of Illinois at Chicago found that emotional intelligence positively impacts ethical decision-making. The study revealed that individuals with higher emotional intelligence were more likely to consider the ethical implications of their actions and make choices that aligned with social responsibility principles.

- *Benefits of Emotional Intelligence for Social Responsibility*
- *Improved understanding of how actions impact others*
- *Increased empathy and consideration for others' perspectives*
- *Enhanced ability to make ethical decisions*
- *Contribution to ethical leadership and positive human relations*

Overall, emotional intelligence is a vital aspect of social responsibility. By developing and cultivating emotional intelligence, individuals and organizations can promote ethical behavior, enhance interpersonal relationships, and positively impact society.

**Case Study: Emotional Intelligence in Practice**

An example of emotional intelligence in action can be seen in the leadership of *Satya Nadella*, the CEO of Microsoft. Nadella's emphasis on empathy and emotional intelligence has transformed the company's culture, fostering a greater focus on social responsibility. Under Nadella's leadership, Microsoft has committed to reducing its carbon footprint, fostering diversity and inclusion, and providing technology access to underserved communities. By incorporating emotional intelligence into his leadership approach, Nadella has not only improved Microsoft's ethical practices but also positioned the company as a leader in social responsibility.

**The Role of Ethics, Social Responsibility, and Emotional Intelligence**

Ethics, social responsibility, and emotional intelligence are interconnected concepts that significantly impact personal and organizational behavior. When individuals and organizations prioritize these aspects, they create a more ethical and responsible environment that fosters positive human relations.

Better ethical decision-making and social responsibility efforts can be achieved by improving emotional intelligence. Emotional intelligence encompasses self-awareness, self-management, social awareness, and relationship management, enabling individuals to make ethical choices that consider the well-being of others and the broader community.

By embracing ethics and social responsibility, individuals and organizations demonstrate a commitment to doing what is right and just. Ethical individuals value principles such as honesty, integrity, and fairness, while ethical organizations integrate social responsibility into their core values, policies, and practices.

| Ethics | Social Responsibility | Emotional Intelligence | Human Relations |
|---|---|---|---|
| Prioritizes moral principles and values | Considers the impact of actions on society | Enhances self-awareness and empathy | Fosters positive interactions and teamwork |
| Guides decision-making processes | Addresses environmental, social, and economic concerns | Enables self-regulation and effective communication | Builds trust, respect, and collaboration |
| Shapes organizational culture | Encourages philanthropic initiatives | Develops social awareness and leadership skills | Nurtures a supportive and inclusive work environment |

Together, these factors contribute to the development of ethical leaders who advocate for social responsibility and establish positive human relations within organizations. When ethics, social responsibility, and emotional intelligence are prioritized, it creates a framework for ethical decision-making, responsible actions, and a harmonious workplace.

**The Link Between Business Communication and Social Responsibility**

Business communication plays a significant role in demonstrating an organization's commitment to social responsibility. Effective communication practices go beyond conveying messages; they also involve ethical considerations and awareness of the societal impact of communication. By aligning communication policies, correspondence, slogans, and corporate credos with ethical and socially responsible principles, businesses can project an image of integrity and accountability.

Interaction with various stakeholders, including other organizations, the government, the press, and the public, should also reflect ethical standards and social responsibility. Engaging in open and transparent communication fosters trust and builds positive relationships, while considering the wider implications of communication ensures that messages are responsible, respectful, and promote the well-being of society.

Social responsibility and corporate ethics are vital elements in today's business landscape. In an ever-evolving society, companies and individuals are expected to carefully consider the impact of their actions and make ethical decisions that benefit not only themselves but also the wider community.

The growing emphasis on social responsibility has prompted the establishment of ethical codes and guidelines for businesses. These guidelines serve as essential frameworks for organizations to navigate the complex ethical landscape and make informed choices that align with societal expectations. By prioritizing ethical behavior, companies can build trust, foster loyalty, and maintain a positive reputation in the eyes of their stakeholders.

Furthermore, ethical leadership plays a significant role in driving social responsibility within organizations. Leaders who demonstrate strong ethical principles and lead by example inspire their teams to follow suit. With ethical leaders at the helm, organizations are better equipped to navigate ethical challenges and contribute positively to society.

As businesses continue to recognize their impact on society, the importance of social responsibility and corporate ethics will only increase. It is crucial for organizations and individuals alike to integrate ethical decision-making into their everyday practices, fostering a culture where social responsibility is a priority. By doing so, they can contribute to a more ethical and sustainable future for all.

# Future-Proofing
# Your Venture

Welcome to Chapter 20 of our book. In this chapter, we delve into the strategies and insights you need for future-proofing your venture in a rapidly evolving market. As the business landscape continues to change at an unprecedented pace, it is crucial to stay ahead of the curve and position your venture for long-term success.

With investment-ready insights and a deep understanding of emerging tech trends, you can navigate the challenges and uncertainties that lie ahead. By adapting to the ever-changing business environment, you ensure that your venture remains resilient and can thrive in the face of disruption.

Let's explore the key strategies that can help you future-proof your venture, from embracing innovative technologies to anticipating market shifts. By staying at the forefront of industry trends and proactively adjusting your business strategy, you can position your venture as not just adaptable but truly investment-ready.

Throughout this chapter, we will provide practical advice and valuable insights from industry experts and successful entrepreneurs who have navigated the rapidly evolving market. From making critical decisions to embracing change, we will cover a wide range of topics that are vital for the long-term success of your venture.

So, strap in and get ready to gain the knowledge and tools you need to future-proof your venture and excel in the dynamic world of business. Let's dive into the exciting realm of future-proofing, investment readiness, and the latest tech trends!

**Understanding the Decision to Pursue or Pull the Plug**

One of the critical decisions entrepreneurs face is whether to pursue their venture or pull the plug. This decision point often arises when entrepreneurs evaluate their future prospects, including cash flow and their faith in the venture.

When evaluating the future of your venture, it's crucial to consider various factors. Let's take a look at some key elements to weigh:

*Cash Flow:* Evaluate the financial health of your business. Are you generating sufficient revenue to sustain operations? Assessing your cash flow will provide insights into the financial viability of your venture.

*Faith in the Venture:* Consider your confidence in the success of your venture. Reflect on your passion and belief in the potential of your business. Assess whether you still possess the drive and motivation to overcome obstacles and pursue your entrepreneurial vision.

By carefully evaluating these factors, you can reach a decision that aligns with your goals and future aspirations. It's essential to remember that this decision is crucial for the future of your venture and should not be taken lightly.

**The Importance of Thinking Ahead**

When embarking on your entrepreneurial journey, it's crucial to think ahead and consider your long-term goals. While it's important to focus on the present, thinking about what comes after the venture and planning for the future can position your business for long-term success.

Thinking ahead involves envisioning the possibilities that lie beyond your current venture. It's about setting your sights on the next chapter in your entrepreneurial journey and planning for the future plans and career transitions that may arise along the way.

By thinking ahead and setting long-term goals, you can align your actions and decisions with your vision for the future. This proactive approach allows you to make strategic choices that will benefit your venture and help you navigate the ever-evolving business landscape.

Considering what comes after the venture is also essential. Building a successful business doesn't necessarily mean staying with it forever. Many entrepreneurs eventually reach a point where they decide to move on to new ventures or explore different career paths.

By thinking ahead and planning for these possibilities, you can ensure a smooth transition and capitalize on the skills and experiences gained during your entrepreneurial journey. Whether it's starting a new venture, joining a different industry, or pursuing a corporate role, thinking ahead prepares you for the future and opens doors to new opportunities.

In summary, thinking ahead and considering your long-term goals is crucial in your entrepreneurial journey. It allows you to anticipate future challenges and opportunities, adapt to changes, and make informed decisions that align with your vision. So, take the time to think ahead and plan for what comes after the venture – your future self will thank you.

**Shifting Perspectives on Entrepreneurship**

Entrepreneurship is a journey that spans different seasons in our careers. Rather than viewing it as a linear path, it can be helpful to see our lives and careers as a series of interconnected chapters. Shifting perspectives in entrepreneurship allows us to navigate professional challenges with a strategic mindset and make informed career decisions.

By embracing the concept of different seasons, we can adapt to the ever-changing landscape of entrepreneurship. Just like the changing seasons, each phase in our career presents unique opportunities and challenges. Whether we are in a season of growth, exploration, or consolidation, understanding the dynamics of each phase can guide our decisions and actions.

One way to approach entrepreneurship with a shifting perspective is by building a career portfolio. Instead of focusing solely on one venture or job, diversifying our experiences can provide valuable insights and enhance our professional growth. By broadening our skill sets and knowledge through different projects and roles, we become more adaptable and resilient in the face of challenges.

Professional challenges are inevitable in entrepreneurship, but they should not deter us from pursuing our goals. Instead, they should be seen as opportunities for growth and learning. By embracing these challenges, we can develop valuable skills and capabilities that will serve us well in future endeavors.

**Shifting Perspectives in Entrepreneurship**

| Seasons | Key Characteristics | Opportunities | Challenges |
|---------|--------------------|--------------|-----------|
| Season of Growth | Rapid expansion, innovation | New market opportunities, scaling | Resource constraints, operational hurdles |
| Season of Exploration | Experimentation, market research | Discovering untapped markets, product development | Uncertainty, initial investment risks |
| Season of Consolidation | Stabilization, optimization | Improving efficiency, streamlining operations | Competitive pressures, market saturation |

This table showcases the different seasons in entrepreneurship, highlighting their key characteristics, opportunities, and challenges. It provides a framework for understanding the shifting nature of our entrepreneurial journey and how we can navigate each season effectively. By adopting a shifting perspective on entrepreneurship, we can embrace the diverse experiences and challenges that come our way. This mindset allows us to adapt, grow, and make strategic career decisions that align with our long-term goals.

**Leveraging Entrepreneurial Experience in a Corporate Role**

Entrepreneurial experience is a valuable asset when transitioning to a corporate leadership role. The skills and mindset acquired from building new businesses and creating innovative solutions can bring significant value to a corporate setting. In today's rapidly evolving business landscape, corporate leaders of the 21st century need to embrace the mindset of creators and innovators to drive growth and stay ahead of the competition.

As an entrepreneur, you have likely faced numerous challenges and uncertainties. These experiences have sharpened your problem-solving skills and ability to adapt to change. In a corporate role, this entrepreneurial experience can be leveraged to drive positive change, foster a culture of innovation, and identify new opportunities for the organization.

One area where entrepreneurial experience can be particularly valuable is in building new businesses within a larger corporate structure. The ability to identify market gaps, develop strategic plans, and execute on innovative business ideas is often crucial for driving growth and diversification.

**A Case Study in Leveraging Entrepreneurial Experience**

Let's take a look at the case of Amy Johnson, who transitioned from running her own successful startup to a leadership role at a large technology company. Amy's entrepreneurial experience provided her with a unique perspective and set of skills that enabled her to make a significant impact in her new corporate role.

| Key Skills and Experiences | Value-Add in Corporate Role |
|---|---|
| Experience in building and scaling a startup | Expertise in driving growth and innovation strategies |
| Ability to adapt quickly to changing market dynamics | Agility in navigating industry disruptions and identifying new opportunities |
| Strong problem-solving and decision-making skills | Efficiency in addressing complex challenges and driving strategic initiatives |
| Entrepreneurial mindset and risk-taking attitude | Encouragement of a culture of innovation and experimentation |

Amy's entrepreneurial experience allowed her to bring a fresh perspective to the corporate world and challenge conventional thinking. She built cross-functional teams, fostered a culture of collaboration and creativity, and introduced new approaches to problem-solving. Her value-add extended beyond her specific role and positively impacted the entire organization.

**Embracing the Mindset of Creators and Innovators**

In today's fast-paced business environment, corporate leaders need to embrace the mindset of creators and innovators. This means actively seeking out new opportunities, encouraging a culture of experimentation, and being open to calculated risks. By leveraging their entrepreneurial experience, corporate leaders can drive innovation, adapt to change, and position their organizations for long-term success.

By tapping into the entrepreneurial spirit within the corporate setting, leaders can inspire their teams to think creatively, challenge the status quo, and continuously seek opportunities for growth. This mindset shift can be a catalyst for building a culture of innovation, attracting top talent, and staying ahead in a highly competitive market.

In conclusion, leveraging entrepreneurial experience in a corporate role is a strategic advantage for both individuals and organizations. The skills, mindset, and value-add that entrepreneurs bring to the table can drive growth, foster innovation, and position companies for success in the modern business landscape. Embracing the mindset of creators and innovators is no longer an option but a necessity for corporate leaders of the 21st century.

## Dealing with Second Guessing and Self-Doubt

When it comes to making significant career transitions, it's only natural to experience second-guessing and self-doubt. The fear of the unknown and the uncertainty of the future can often leave us feeling unsure about the decisions we make. But it's important to remember that self-doubt is a common part of personal growth and embracing change.

Instead of letting self-doubt consume us, we can adopt strategies to deal with these emotions and move forward with confidence. Here are a few suggestions:

### 1. Seek Support and Guidance

Reach out to mentors, coaches, or trusted friends who can provide guidance and support during this transitional phase. They can offer advice, share their own experiences, and provide the reassurance you may need to overcome self-doubt.

### 2. Focus on Personal Growth

Use this opportunity for personal growth and self-reflection. Take time to assess your strengths, skills, and values. Set goals and identify areas where you can develop and improve. By focusing on personal growth, you can build confidence and align your career decisions with your true aspirations.

### 3. Embrace Change as an Opportunity

Instead of viewing career transitions as daunting challenges, embrace them as opportunities for growth and new experiences. Remember that change is a constant in life, and by embracing it, you open yourself up to exciting possibilities and the chance to expand your horizons.

### 4. Trust Your Instincts

Listen to your intuition and trust in your ability to make the right decisions for yourself. While it's essential to seek advice and guidance, ultimately, you know yourself better than anyone else. Trust that you have the skills, knowledge, and resilience to navigate your chosen path.

By implementing these strategies, you can overcome second-guessing and self-doubt and embrace change with confidence. Remember, career transitions are opportunities for personal growth and aligning your career with your current season of life. Trust yourself, and believe that you have what it takes to succeed.

## Lessons from an Executive Turned VC Tech Investor

In this section, we will delve into the insights of Eash Sundaram, a former Chief Information Officer (CIO) who transitioned into the world of Venture Capital (VC) as a tech investor. Sundaram's career journey is a testament to the turning points and career transitions that can lead professionals to venture capital, startup acceleration, and board leadership.

As a CIO, Sundaram gained extensive experience in navigating the intersection of technology and business strategy. This experience became the catalyst for his career transition into the world of venture capital, where he could use his industry knowledge and expertise to identify promising startups and fuel their growth.

As an investor and startup accelerator, CIOs like Sundaram can bring unique value to the world of venture capital. Their deep understanding of technology and the challenges faced by startups makes them insightful partners in investment decisions and strategic guidance.

Sundaram's journey also showcases the importance of actively participating in board leadership roles. As a board leader, he has gained valuable insights into the inner workings of startups, allowing him to guide and shape their trajectory for success.

Sundaram's Key Career Transitions and Achievements

| Career Transition | Achievements |
| --- | --- |
| CIO in the Technology Industry | Provided strategic direction and managed complex technology initiatives within Fortune 500 companies. |
| Transition to VC Tech Investor | Used industry expertise to identify and invest in high-potential tech startups, supporting their growth and success. |
| Board Leadership | Guided and shaped the trajectory of startups as a board leader, leveraging his deep industry knowledge. |

Through Sundaram's career transitions, we can gain valuable insights into the power of venture capital, the importance of startup acceleration, and the role of board leadership in driving success. His experiences shed light on the journey from executive roles to VC investor and exemplify the value that professionals from diverse backgrounds bring to the ever-evolving world of startups and innovation.

## The Impact of Cybersecurity Incidents on Business Strategy

In today's digital landscape, cybersecurity incidents pose significant threats to businesses worldwide. In this section, we will analyze the impact of such incidents, with a particular focus on supply chain attacks, on business strategy. We will explore the importance of maintaining robust infrastructure security, staying current on software upgrades, and implementing effective security measures. Through a deep dive into a high-profile cyber incident, we will uncover invaluable lessons learned and strategies for managing and mitigating future attacks.

## The Increasing Significance of Cybersecurity

Cybersecurity incidents are no longer isolated occurrences but have emerged as key considerations for businesses across industries. The rapid digitization and interconnectivity of systems have made organizations vulnerable to various types of attacks, including supply chain attacks. These attacks exploit weaknesses in the supply chain of software products and can have far-reaching consequences on businesses, from financial loss to reputational damage.

It is crucial for companies to prioritize infrastructure security to safeguard their networks, systems, and data. By implementing layers of protection, businesses can create a robust defense against potential cyber threats. This includes adopting industry best practices, conducting regular vulnerability assessments, and investing in advanced threat detection and response mechanisms.

## The Role of Software Upgrades in Mitigating Cyber Risks

Staying current on software upgrades is vital for maintaining a secure business infrastructure. Software vendors constantly release updates that not only enhance functionality but also address vulnerabilities discovered along the way. Failure to implement these upgrades leaves businesses exposed to known security risks and increases the likelihood of successful cyber attacks.

In addition to regularly updating systems and applications, organizations should establish a comprehensive approach to software security. This includes systematically testing software for vulnerabilities, engaging in code reviews, and conducting ongoing risk assessments. By prioritizing software security throughout the development lifecycle, businesses can prevent potential breaches and minimize the impact of cyber incidents.

**Creating a Table to Showcase Cybersecurity Incidents and Their Impact**

| Cybersecurity Incident | Impact on Businesses |
|---|---|
| NotPetya Ransomware Attack | Caused billions of dollars in damages, disrupting global supply chains and affecting companies in various sectors, highlighting the need for robust cybersecurity measures. |
| SolarWinds Supply Chain Attack | Exposed vulnerabilities in supply chain security, compromising the networks of numerous government agencies and companies, emphasizing the importance of supply chain risk management. |
| WannaCry Ransomware Attack | Infected hundreds of thousands of computers worldwide, causing significant disruptions in healthcare, logistics, and manufacturing industries, reinforcing the necessity of proactive cybersecurity measures. |

**Lessons Learned and Strategies for Mitigating Cybersecurity Incidents**

Through analyzing high-profile cyber incidents, businesses can gain valuable insights and develop strategies to better protect themselves from similar attacks. Some key takeaways include:

- Implementing a multi-layered security approach to defend against a wide range of cyber threats.
- Establishing policies and procedures for software upgrades and patches to stay ahead of vulnerabilities.
- Investing in employee training and awareness programs to enhance cybersecurity hygiene.
- Regularly conducting threat assessments and penetration tests to identify and address vulnerabilities.
- Engaging with trusted cybersecurity experts for guidance and support in managing risks.

By incorporating these lessons into their business strategies, organizations can fortify their defenses and mitigate the impact of potential cybersecurity incidents, ensuring the security and continuity of their operations.

**The Success and Challenges of CRM Strategies**

In today's rapidly evolving business landscape, CRM strategies play a crucial role in driving customer relationship management and fostering business growth. However, they also come with their own set of challenges. Let's explore the success and challenges associated with CRM strategies and how businesses are adapting to overcome them.

**The Impact of CRM Trends and AI Advances**

The field of CRM is constantly evolving, with new trends and advancements emerging regularly. These trends include the integration of artificial intelligence (AI) into CRM systems, enabling businesses to leverage advanced analytics and automation capabilities to enhance customer interactions and streamline processes. AI-powered CRM solutions offer predictive analytics and personalized recommendations, enabling businesses to deliver targeted marketing campaigns and cater to individual customer needs.

AI advances have significantly improved CRM capabilities, allowing businesses to analyze vast amounts of customer data in real-time and gain valuable insights. This not only helps in identifying trends and patterns but also enables businesses to proactively engage with customers, drive sales, and provide exceptional customer experiences.

**Expanding Data Capabilities and Process Automation**

Data is the backbone of CRM strategies, and businesses today have access to large volumes of customer data from various sources. With expanding data capabilities, businesses can effectively segment their customer base, personalize communication, and deliver tailored experiences. This enables businesses to build stronger relationships with customers and drive customer loyalty.

Additionally, process automation plays a crucial role in CRM strategies by streamlining repetitive tasks, reducing manual effort, and improving efficiency. Automation allows businesses to focus on high-value activities that require human intervention while automating routine tasks such as data entry, lead scoring, and follow-up reminders. This not only saves time but also ensures consistency and accuracy in customer interactions.

## Overcoming Challenges and Driving Business Growth

While CRM strategies offer numerous benefits, businesses often face challenges in their implementation and adoption. Common challenges include data quality and integration issues, resistance to change, and ensuring user adoption across the organization. Overcoming these challenges requires a comprehensive approach that encompasses data governance, user training, and change management strategies.

To drive business growth through CRM strategies, it is essential for businesses to align their CRM initiatives with their overall business goals. This involves defining clear objectives, implementing the right CRM tools and technologies, and regularly monitoring and measuring the effectiveness of CRM efforts. By continuously refining and optimizing their CRM strategies, businesses can improve customer satisfaction, increase sales, and achieve sustainable growth.

The key to future-proofing your venture lies in implementing effective strategies that allow you to adapt to change and embrace emerging tech trends. In today's rapidly evolving market, staying ahead requires a proactive approach and a willingness to explore new possibilities.

By prioritizing future-proofing strategies, you can ensure that your business is well-positioned for the challenges and opportunities that lie ahead. This includes investing in technologies that have the potential to revolutionize your industry, cultivating a culture of innovation and adaptability, and continually evaluating your business model to identify areas for improvement. Moreover, being investment-ready is essential for attracting the necessary funding to drive your venture forward. Investors are looking for businesses that have embraced change and are prepared for the future, which makes implementing these strategies crucial. By demonstrating your commitment to staying ahead of the curve, you can enhance your credibility and increase your chances of securing the investment you need to fuel growth.

# A Few Final Words..

In closing, this book has explored the many facets of building a successful business in today's dynamic environment. We have covered essential topics such as financial projections, risk mitigation strategies, market analysis, and future-proofing your venture.

The takeaway is that success requires agility, strategic thinking, and the ability to adapt to change. Businesses must cultivate a proactive mindset, evaluating their models continuously and seeking opportunities to stay ahead of emerging trends.

While challenges will arise, those who persevere with resilience, creativity and a vision for long-term growth will position themselves to surmount obstacles. By strengthening their foundations through responsible planning and diligent execution of tactics, organizations can navigate uncertainties with confidence as they ascend towards new heights.

This book serves as a guide on the expedition towards sustaining your entrepreneurial endeavor. The journey ahead includes twists, turns and unforeseen situations that call for constant learning, open-mindedness and a resolute dedication to goals. Let the insights shared here serve to illuminate the pathways ahead as you steer your venture skillfully through both calms and storms.

Above all, remember that lasting success stems from an intrinsic drive to continuously challenge limits, adapt fast and deliver value to others. With the right mindset and practical strategies, the future remains yours to shape as you elevate your venture to its fullest potential.

*"The biggest risk of all, is in not taking one."*

# Further Reading and Bibliography

Porter, M. E., & Kramer, M. R. (2011, January). Creating shared value. Harvard Business Review.

Davison, M. (2011, October 13). The challenges of change management. CIO.

Poon, N. T. (2020, October 2). An ethical dilemma checklist for decision-making. Greater Good Magazine.

Gallo, C. (2014, November 10). The value of failure. Harvard Business Review.

Barrington, L. (2019, June). The future of jobs and skills in 2030. World Economic Forum.

Rowsell-Jones, A. (2021, August 25). What are the challenges of business growth? Investopedia.

Turner, A. (2020, September 14). 6 tips for choosing startup investors. Entrepreneur.

Andreassen, T. W., Lervik-Olsen, L., Snyder, H., van Vaerenbergh, Y., Holmbeck, G. N., & Shurtleff, D. (2016). Business students' choice of communication channels: Effects of media richness and social presence. Journal of Business and Technical Communication, 31(1), 67–96.